I0839748

DC LAW

Door County Land Air Water

SD Press

2073 County Trunk Dk
Brussels, Wisconsin 54204
bhanson@southerndoor.k12.wi.us

Copyright © 2018
Southern Door High School
Adviser: Brett Hanson
All rights reserved.

Acknowledgement and permissions granted.
Cover design by Emily Koelpien.

ISBN-13: 978-1984375063
ISBN-10: 1984375067
   1.   Land. 2. Air 3. Water

Printed in the United States of America.
LIBRARY OF CONGRESS CATALOGING-IN-PUBLICATION DATA

"A heartfelt examination of the natural beauty and fragility of the Door Peninsula ecosystem as experienced by its most precious resource...our children. The passages contained herein are written with a concern for the present and a healthy dose of optimism for the future."
—David Samuels
Southern Door High School Science Teacher

Table of Contents

Introduction
Written by Gracie Englebert

Each summer, Door County residents as well as tourists from around the country flock to the lookout tower at Potawatomi State Park. From the top of the tower, you feel as if you can see for miles beyond Small and Big Islands, beyond the stone quarry across Sturgeon Bay, all the way to the point where the limitless sky merges with the endless water. A soft, warm breeze, ever present at the top of the 225-foot tower, carries the subtle smell of the bay as well as the soft calls of songbirds filling the trees. After running on the miles of trails through the park, I often scale the steep steps to the top. Each time, without fail, the sights, sounds, and smells at the top of the tower allow me to escape the commotion of everyday life and experience nature in its most untouched and ethereal form.

In a world that seems to move faster each day, it's easy to overlook the beauty of nature and to dismiss our responsibility to protect the land, air, and water that sustain us. We habitually choose the easiest, fastest, or cheapest option, disregarding the indisputable impact our actions have on the environment. However, in a time when rainforests continue to give way to concrete jungles, it is paramount that we protect the unblemished beauty of our home, Door County.

While many of the contributors to DC LAW will be leaving Door County in the next year or two, it will always remain our home. Perhaps this is why we feel responsible to advocate for the well-being of our environment, but I believe our dedication emanates from somewhere more intimate. This reason, unique to each of us, stems from a personal relationship with Mother Nature—one we've been able to enhance through our work with DC LAW. While I fear even our best writing will fail to capture the essence of this relationship, I hope our passion and commitment to the environment will inspire you to reflect on your own unique relationship with the natural world around you.

Each year, for the past twelve years, the Great World Texts program has chosen a classic piece of literature for high school students and teachers to interpret. In preparation for Southern Door's participation in the program, our AP Literature class has chosen to compose and publish (in conjunction with the English 11 Honors students) an original book inspired by the 2018 designated text, *Silent Spring*. Based on Rachel Carson's revolutionary non-fiction book, we have addressed the many environmental issues plaguing Door County. Just as Carson's work was said to have spurred the environmental movement, we hope our work with DC LAW will spur a movement in our home county.

Over the past several months, we have worked to present Door County's environmental issues through our research and writing as well as with our online presence through our website. Many of the compositions also include ways for our readers to help combat these problems. I am confident that many of the contributors to DC LAW will go on to live more mindfully, and it is our hope that the readers of this book will be inspired to do the same.

The Environmental Declaration of the Citizens of Door County

Written by Megan Neubauer

When in the course of time it becomes necessary for dedicated citizens to ensure their environmental rights, and to assume the voice of the natural earth, it is imperative that we clarify what is environmentally just for the sake of Mother Nature and her children.

Therefore, we hold these truths to be self evident: Mother Nature deserves respect, compassion, and protection, and all elements of nature are created equal. It is our duty, as ethical citizens, to institute these ideals immediately and consistently. Furthermore, Citizens must protest the irresponsible actions of corporations and neglectful citizens to protect our beautiful environment. Whenever the environment suffers from destructive changes, society must restore the natural world and protect the following Environmental Rights:

The Right to Witness the Change of Seasons:
Door County citizens insist on the protection of our colorful foliage. Door County's change of seasons is crucial to environmentalists and business owners. The phenomenon of our parks experiencing four unique seasons should be promised for future generations. The removal of our seasons through global warming and emissions will be prohibited.

The Right to Natural Solutions:

 The residents of Door County need to participate in only natural experiments. While the overpopulation of certain animals occurs naturally, many scientists are using gene alterations to rid the earth of these overpopulated species. Because of the unpredictability of these experiments, unforeseen, detrimental effects occur. By refusing to allow fabricated experiments, our environment will be safe from any unnatural havoc.

The Right to Fresh Drinking Water:

 Door County inhabitants demand fresh drinking water free from manure. Manure spreading policies in Door County need to change. As the result of heavy rainfall, runoff manure works its way into our streams, rivers, lakes, and eventually our groundwater. Contaminated groundwater infects wells like an epidemic, affecting more wells each year. Large farms and factories contributing to the destruction of our wells will not be tolerated.

The Right to a Habitat that will Endure for Years to Come:

 The citizens of Door County demand natural habitats for the preservation of wildlife. With our booming tourism industry, Door County's habitats need the locals' protection. The Door County Land Trusts must be protected and more habitats must be saved before people do not remember what natural Door County looks like anymore. Because Door County calls itself a "bird-watching zone," the preservation of our plethora of bird species is of utmost importance. By protecting land from industrialization, we will avoid losing Door County's many species.

15

The Right to Breathe Air Free From Pollutants:

Door County residents expect clean, fresh smelling air. While many tourists reside full time in heavily polluted cities, vacationing in fresh-air Door County makes for a memorable experience. This rare, fresh air characteristic needs to be protected from the growing popularity of air-polluting recreational activities and the excessive use of cars moving to and from the pristine peninsula. Door County will reject the use of excessive air pollutants.

The Right to Enjoy Clean Beaches:

The inhabitants of Door County must prioritize the beaches. Because Door County is a peninsula, beaches surround us on three of four sides. People are meant to enjoy these beaches; however, it is important to remember to keep them free from waste and garbage. These iconic shores are a beautiful landmark that generations to come want to enjoy, and they will, with the help of caring citizens. Door County disapproves misusing beaches and natural shores.

The Right to Protect Our Future Generations:

Door County citizens must protect future generations. In fact, we deserve the knowledge that generations to come will grow up in the beautiful, healthy environment we grew up in. Our children are entitled to an environment as chemical-free as possible, and through the preservation of our environment, Door County will continue to be an outstanding place to raise families. Door County will not allow our children to be harmed by a toxic environment.

The Right to Experience the Sounds of Nature:

The residents of Door County insist on enjoying all the sounds of nature. For years to come, people should experience the singing birds in the morning, the buzzing bees in the afternoon, and the chirping frogs at night. These unique natural sounds add acoustic beauty to our aesthetic county. Door County refuses to let our natural sounds disappear.

The Right to Enjoy the Night Skies:

Door County inhabitants must care for the night skies. In Door County, bright, vibrant stars have always dotted the vast open skies. With the increase of light pollution due to the growing popularity of Door County vacation homes, the stars have started to disappear. As Door County citizens, it's important to reserve the right to enjoy the true beauty of the stars. Door County will not condone the extinction of the stars.

The Right to Use Natural Pesticides:

The citizens of Door County have the option to use natural pesticides. While around the world synthetic pesticides are becoming increasingly popular, Door County needs to refuse to use synthetic pesticides. Natural pesticides allow nature to do its job and run its course by managing a population without damning species to local extinction. Door County does not stand for the use of synthetic pesticides or any of their derivatives.

In conclusion, representatives to this county will cherish its natural state and will rally around these rights with full confidence. They will publish and declare that Door County's environment is protected by its caring residents. Independence *from the neglecting ways of society ought to be recognized by all of Door County. By declaring what's important to Mother Nature, the citizens of Door County gain the right to enjoy all aspects of land, air, water, and all natural elements in between. This document ensures that our past, our present, and our future in Door County's beautiful landscape will endure for generations.*

LAND

"To waste, to destroy our natural resources, to skin and exhaust the land instead of using it so as to increase its usefulness, will result in undermining in the days of our children the very prosperity which we ought by right to hand down to them amplified and developed."
—Theodore Roosevelt
Naturalist and 26th President of The United States

Environmental Laws in Door County

Written by Regan Norton

Today's government is focused on borders and national security. It's focused on our controversial new president, healthcare, and tax reform. When was the last time you heard anything about our environment on the news? When was the last time your radio informed you of the laws pertaining to our groundwater or waste management? Many laws in the Door County area concerning environmental issues are outdated or demand better regulation, calling for residents to become more informed. Door County's population is now faced with a difficult decision due to several budding problems desperately in need of a solution, including our loss of power to control Shoreland

Zoning, the pollution of groundwater, and the preservation of our home's natural beauty. We need to be better informed on what laws we have in place protecting our environment, what can be done to update and improve said laws, and what deems these changes feasible.

Currently, the ordinances in Door County are outdated and nonspecific to our county. The Door County Shoreland Zoning Ordinance, created in 1968, is a prime example. Enacted for the efficient use of Door County's water resources, it granted the county the power to regulate the use of shorelands to prevent water pollution. Due to the abundance of shoreline in Door County, it proved essential that we implemented strict laws for the general welfare of our county. Since then, our power has been withdrawn by the state of Wisconsin through the passages of Act 55 and Act 170. Act 55 represses the additional regulation of the construction and maintenance of buildings on the shore that is not explicitly expressed in the shoreland zoning standards. Similarly, Act 170 grants additional freedoms to private property owners when public safety should remain the primary focus. These acts inhibit local control, the very location where it is likely to prove effective. The Door County Environmental Council accounts for just one of many organizations calling for awareness to regain power from the state.

Another prevalent issue within Door County remains the heavy ground and surface water pollution. The Door County Environmental Council identified the undeniable phosphorus pollution within Northeastern Wisconsin, as well as several sources of this problem. Although failing septic systems and lawn fertilizers undoubtedly contribute to the contamination, an overwhelming amount of evidence proves that poor manure management from concentrated animal feeding operations, or CAFOs, is one of the larger factors causing the contamination of our water supply. A single cow produces approximately eighteen times the amount of waste that a human does. This means that a CAFO with four thousand cows produces an amount of waste equivalent to a city with a population of seventy-two thousand people, or approximately one thousand more people than the population of Eau Claire, Wisconsin. However, unlike our cities, these CAFOs do not have efficient and environmentally friendly ways to dispose of this waste, leaving them to spray it on the ground and into the air. Created in 1987, our Agricultural Performance Standards and Animal Waste Storage Ordinance was developed to protect the area's ground and surface water. This ordinance lacks the recognition of the CAFOs in our county that are contaminating our waters. Since there is currently a combined total of eighteen CAFOs in Door and Kewaunee counties, we should focus on regulating these farms. An expansion moratorium or some other type of preventative measure is necessary to ensure water pollution in our county doesn't get out of hand.

A final call to action results from our economy's dependence on the natural beauty of our county. There is no doubt that Door County is a beautiful area, attracting tourists from all over the country. Becoming an active citizen and working to ensure our county thrives for generations to come remains an essential element of living in this area. Therefore, it proves crucial for ordinances, such as the Solid Waste Management regulations, to evolve with the county's environment. This ordinance outlines the authority and responsibilities of the Door County Highway Committee, as well as how citizens dispose of solid waste. It also clearly maps out the penalties of failing to abide by these regulations. Keeping our environment waste-free is essential for an aesthetically pleasing home. However, this ordinance was written in 1998, nearly twenty years ago. When dealing with something so important, we need an updated reassessment of our waste management, and stricter laws to keep our county clean. Door County and its residents maintain a relationship described as nothing less than interdependent. This means our county's environment depends on the population to care for and protect it, just as we citizens place our lives in the hands of our environment. Not only do we rely on the environment to provide needs as simple, yet crucial, as water and land for agriculture, but also for concepts as complex as the beauty that drives our economy and allows us to thrive.

This being said, it remains the right and responsibility of citizens to stay informed of the regulations on our environment. We hold the power to change our home for the better or worse. It is our obligation to change and develop ordinances in order to preserve our environment. Once we identify the key problems within Door County, our population needs to follow through with the implementation of new laws that specifically address these issues. Whether this means reclaiming Shoreland Zoning power from the state for better local control, changing our waste management rules to ensure that our water is clean and usable, or saving our economy through the preservation of our gorgeous county, we must address the issues and follow through for the good of our home.

As stated in Rachel Carson's *Silent Spring*, "The public must decide whether it wishes to continue on the present road, and it can do so only when in full possession of the facts." She also includes a quote by Jean Rostand: "The obligation to endure gives us the right to know." Due to our interdependent relationship with the environment, it is the obligation of all individuals to familiarize themselves with how our county is currently being protected. Not only this, but it is also crucial that we help develop evolved environmental regulations to protect the future.

Today's government is focused on borders and national security. It's focused on our controversial new president, healthcare, and tax reform, but nothing is as important as our environment; without it we wouldn't have borders to protect, a president to govern, lives to care for, or an economy to regulate. Door County has many environmental issues easily corrected by the creation and enforcement of rules to conserve our county's precious natural beauty. We as citizens need to update regulations and abide by them to ensure *our* spring will not be silenced, as Rachel Carson predicted in the book that sparked the entire environmental movement.

Fighting for our Forests

Nature's Necessities

Written By Erin Tadych

The forest in my backyard is consumed in flames,
I watch, admiring its beauty.
Each leaf stained a vivid orange-yellow—oh look at
the glow!
Except for the pines who haven't been harmed.
Their hard composition provides shelter and
warmth

For my beating heart.
They're purposeful for
The life of every living thing on this planet—human
and not.

Notebooks, cups, magazines, calendars, books,
fishing poles, pencils, tables, and houses.
Materialistic,
Yet recreational.
Of everyone in Door County,
Many are hunters and fishers.
Trees provide a home for my neighbor's hunting
stand,
Camouflaging him well.
Later he is rewarded with a big buck,
His prized possession.
With that said,
Many people find happiness with nature.

I like to consider myself lucky
Because I can say I am Earth.
Are we not
Dust, dirt, water, and air?
Are we not
Completely surrounded by nature
Including everything we have made from nature?
Quite fortunate for what we are, yes?
What a shame—we cause it damage
With our technology, chemicals, pollution, and
more.

29

If I am Earth,
Why am I harming myself, too?
If I am Earth,
Why can't I cease the damage?

If we are Earth,
We must save ourselves.

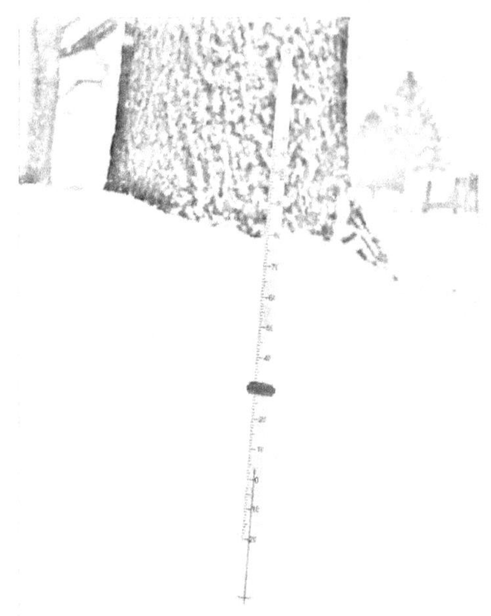

We Are the Solution

Written by Olivia VanDenHeuvel

"Leave your stress behind and relax in simple tranquility. Welcome to Door County, Wisconsin. Treasured by visitors and locals alike, Door County is located in the Midwest within a 4-6-hour drive from Chicago and Minneapolis. With 300 miles of scenic shoreline, 5 state parks, 19 county parks, 11 lighthouses, and 53 public beaches, outdoor activities are endless. A truly artistic and cultural community, Door County boasts over 100 art galleries, museums, and performing art venues. We invite you to sample many of our culinary delights, wines, and brews located across our peninsula. In the evening catch a theater performance, listen to live music, or watch a breathtaking sunset on the shores of Lake Michigan. With 19 communities from the bottom of the peninsula to a ferry ride across to Washington Island, we offer many lodging establishments that will make you feel like you're at home. Start planning your Door County vacation today. Both the visitor guide and website offer endless options for activities, events, dining, and lodging. We hope to see you soon in Door County, Wisconsin. The place we call home."

Door County Visitor Bureau's sales pitch accurately sums up how nearly $18,000,000 of tourism-based revenue is pumped into Door County's economy every year. As the perfect attraction, tourism in Door County creates $70,000,000 of labor income that employs over 4,000 residents. Door County ranks seventh out of seventy-two counties in Wisconsin for best public school performance, lowest crime rates, affordable cost of living, abundant job opportunities, and numerous local amenities. While the summary above describes the culture of Door County, it fails to express the abuse our oppressed land has endured for decades.

Most locals are in agreement that Door County is a wonderful place to live, and I am personally grateful for getting to be one of the 9,043

people that live in Sturgeon Bay. In 2009, my mom
traded the University neighborhood of Eau Claire,
Wisconsin for the front yard of Lake Michigan.
Since then, I've taken advantage of Door County's
beautiful 75-mile long and ten-mile wide peninsula.
From bike riding, trail exploring with my dog,
kayaking, paddle boarding, swimming,
snowshoeing, and snow tubing, I've gotten to live
the wonderful Door County life. Therefore, I think
it's about time I pay my dues, and expose the secret
pain my home's landscape has been enduring.

I've witnessed almost ten glorious falls,
winters, springs, and summers in Door County, as
well as countless sunsets and sunrises. Within those
years I've realized it doesn't take a rocket scientist
to notice the gradual environmental changes that
are affecting the terrain here. I've spent too long
complaining about the ever-diminishing ice on our
winter lakeshores and the increasing
disappointment of leaves each autumn to remain
idle any longer. Sturgeon Bay, Wisconsin has
provided me a home that nature has graciously
decorated. Therefore, it is not only my
responsibility to educate myself about the health of
the habitat I live in, but it is also my obligation to
inform others.

Door County holds two 4,000-year-old
biomes—temperate (deciduous) forest and taiga
(boreal) forest. On the Green Bay side of the county,
the temperate forest biome provides the peninsula

33

with maple, beech, oak, hemlock, and basswood
trees. The Lake Michigan side holds the taiga
biome, which adds spruce, fir, and paper birch
trees. Both biomes are designed for seasonal
changes and heavy rainfall. Next to rainforests,
temperate forest biomes are the wettest biome.
Both taiga and temperate forests thrive in wet
environments. Taiga biomes prefer long cold
winters and short cool summers. While temperate
forest are built to withstand similar conditions,
warm weather actually boosts deciduous tree
growth.

In Door County, Lake Michigan enables the
existence of both of these beautiful biomes because
of the "lake effect." The "lake effect" is a
meteorological phenomenon in which moist, warm
air rises from a body of water and collides with dry,
cold air, resulting in many forms of precipitation.

Since the late 1700s, humans have increased
the quantity of carbon dioxide in the air by forty
percent. Industrial production and motorized
vehicles release gases and radiation into the
atmosphere. These gases contribute to acid rain
that damages leaves on trees. Once the leaves have
been affected by acid rain, the reproduction of
seedlings declines. The trees also become more
susceptible to disease and death.

Within the past century, Wisconsin's overall
temperature has increased two degrees Fahrenheit.
Because of climate warming, Lake Michigan's

surface temperature has warmed. A warmer surface temperature creates a warmer "lake effect," which leads to more humidity, warmth, and precipitation. For temperate forests, these are not threatening circumstances. In fact, warmer temperatures can enhance deciduous tree growth as long as steady rainfall is received. On the other hand, once coastal climates warm, the taiga forest tree leaves cannot properly peak in autumn, nor produce normal amounts of seedlings. According to internationally-acclaimed expert in forest ecology and environment studies, Lee Frelich, Ph.D., Door County is near the "last days of our boreal forest."

When researching, it was hard to believe the hard facts of climate change and its effect on Door County. The truth of the matter is that I have seen Lee's prophecies come true, for the nature around me has verified the legitimacy of his facts. This autumn, 2017, has been one of the gloomiest, rainiest, foggiest, colorless, leafless tree falls in the history of my 18-year-long life. I am clinically diagnosing the weather with bipolar disorder, for one day it is wet, cold, and rainy, and the next it is in the upper seventies (°F). The boreal trees around my house appear confused and weakened from the abusive rain storms and intermittent heat flashes they have been subjected to this summer and fall. It is depressing to think that I am a direct instigator of Mother Nature's ongoing abuse. Even more unbearable to realize is that the ugly rainy days and dead, uncolored leaves everywhere in Door County are not Mother Nature's punishment to us, not her call for help, but rather her warning to us.

Now, it is hard to picture Door County without its famous state and county parks filled with campers, bikers, hikers, runners, hunters, sailors, kayakers, canoers, paddle boarders, bird watchers, and tourists. Even more difficult to imagine is that the culprit responsible for the annihilation of our beloved county is you, me, and every human being since the Industrial Revolution. Along with the death of Door County's nature comes the disappearance of scenic drives to locally-owned shops, restaurants, and other hardworking entrepreneurs and their businesses. The economy will pay the price for the crimes we commit against our environment. The declining health of Door County's biomes will force all terrestrial life to adapt.

If the existence of bright green summers and fiery red, orange, and yellow autumn seasons as well as the wildlife inhabiting those forests are irrelevant to you, then, at the very least, the reduction of oxygen produced by our trees may concern you. We depend upon our green friends to live. On average, one tree makes about two hundred sixty pounds of oxygen each year, so taking the health of our forest into account is worth our time. From a tree's perspective, humans are not necessary for survival, and we could disappear into oblivion without a thought. It is clear who should have the upper-hand in the relationship between humans and nature. Alas, humans possess the power to annihilate nature and humanity alike by adding poisons into the environment, or even ending it all with the push of a nuclear button.

Human-made gases have warmed the surface temperature of our planet by one degree Fahrenheit and physically exhausted the atmosphere in the last fifty years. As a result, evaporation occurs more rapidly, which increases humidity and the average rainfall throughout the world. This past autumn in Door County proves these scientific facts to be true.

At the end of the day, you, me, and every human being on this planet are just as much a part of the problem as we can be a part of the solution. The first step is acknowledging the problem's existence. Reading this book is a pretty good start, but sharing it would be even better. The second step is to start and/or join local environmental groups that prioritize Mother Nature while also promoting her health. I strongly urge Door County residents to visit The Door County Climate Change Coalition website for more information, and to become a member. Science is always changing, and staying updated on the now can help teach us how to create a better future. Practices such as recycling, investing in renewable energy resources, carpooling, utilizing public transportation, walking and biking when possible, and participating in any other forms of eco-friendly options are small acts that add up to a better future.

Overall, the majority of educated people understand that global warming is not a myth and that it is more dangerous than any kind of fabrication man has construed. In 2017, a universal consensus was taken amongst environmental researchers, and it was found that 97 percent of our world's climate experts believe that global warming is real, with humans primarily responsible. Additionally, seven out of every ten Americans believe climate change is real and are worried about its effects. Roughly, the same amount of U.S. citizens supported former U.S. President Barack Obama's Clean Power Plan and wanted to remain in the Paris Agreement. Both acts are designed to lower pollutants emitted in the environment in order to reduce climate warming, yet both lack the support of current President Donald J. Trump. On November 16th, 2017, President Trump tweeted, "The concept of global warming was created by and for the Chinese in order to make U.S. manufacturing non-competitive." Although very creative, President Trump's accusations towards climate change have no basis of factual evidence. On top of that, 95 percent of active environmental scientists who publish their objective findings agree the earth is warming, and humans are the ultimate cause. Nevertheless, 174 countries remain a part of the Paris Agreement, but the United States is no longer one of them. Even so, former President Obama's Clean Power Plan as well as other environmental policies passed under the Obama administration still remain in America until President Trump finds a way to revoke these regulations, too.

No matter your political affiliations or personal beliefs on climate change, objective facts prove our planet is warming at a rapid, never-before-seen rate. Denying the reality of our world's current predicament is just as dangerous as knowing the truth of climate warming and not doing anything about it. Humanity cannot afford to elect public officials who refuse to take scientific facts into consideration when in the process of policy making. From the loss of Door County's taiga forests and the increase of precipitation to the astronomical damages on our world's ecosystems, climate change will change the life of every living organism on earth. We take responsibility for our actions and learn from the mistakes we continue to make. The expression, "you get out what you put in," explains the relationship humanity shares with political leaders and planet Earth. If we recklessly release deadly pollutants into our environment without regulations, in return we will gain an environment unable to sustain life. The health of our planet directly impacts the health of humanity. The environment is one of the most relevant topics

on our government's agenda, considering it's
imminent demise is also our own.

Where My Soul Lives

Written by Emily Koelpien

Here in the woods
The cold does little to banish my feelings
Stubbornly, I press on
Hood up
Hands stuffed in pockets

Here in the woods
The distractions melt away
And I'm left
With my core
And the issues that plague my mind

Here in the woods
I find my haven

Where I seek refuge
From the rest of the world
Alone, blissfully

Here in the woods
I escape, trying to outlast the sun
Whose light has left me
Whose warmth has done little
To warm my soul

Here in the woods
The leaves wave at me as I pass
Some try to join me
"Not today," I tell them
This conversation is between the Earth and I

Here in the woods
No one is listening
Except the birds,
The trees, the bugs
The stream

Here in the woods
Nature listens to my problems
To my theatrics
To my ideas
And nature responds

Here in the woods
The sound of crunching autumn leaves

Sounds the same to me
As a rhetoric
"Mmhmm? Oh yeah?"

Here in the woods
I find comfort its beauty
And its generosity
Because when I'm upset
The woods await

The woods await
With a box of tissues
With a steaming cup of tea
With an ear that'll listen

The woods await
With advice
Telling me that it gets better
Waiting to hear the resolution

The woods watch me grow up
The woods teach me about myself
The woods help me find myself
The woods are therapeutic beyond measure

Whenever I need to clear my head
To figure out what's wrong
I meet my soul
Here in the woods

Forests Today, Zero Tomorrow

Written by Tehya Bertrand

    Imagine a peninsula without bright, glamorous, blossoming cherry trees during the spring. Imagine a peninsula without the lovely voices of hundreds of bird species during the summer. Imagine a peninsula without the vibrantly colored leaves dancing in the sky as the gravitational pull tugs them to the ground during the fall. These visions may become reality unless we, the residents of Door County, preserve our ecosystem. We must not remain oblivious to our county's issues, including deforestation, or the environment will contain only buildings and man-made materials. In Door County, deforestation has been a significant issue since the 1860s, due to logging operations and farming. However, based on past experiences, our generation has learned to preserve forests by placing them in land trusts.

Deforestation became a problem in the 1860s when logging grew into a huge industry. At that time, Door County seemed like the perfect place to obtain an abundant quantity of lumber for the paper mills. Loggers chopped down any trees with a diameter larger than sixteen inches for product. The lumber companies also cut down many old-growth, or original, Eastern Hemlocks just to send their bark to leather tanneries in the south. According to the October 2004 issue of the *Wisconsin Natural Resources* magazine, "Surveys conclude that only about one percent of Wisconsin's old-growth forests remain intact." Near the end of the 19th century, the quantity of trees and good quality lumber diminished greatly, forcing the logging business to move out of Door County. The people of Door County originally thought this would help protect the forests, but ironically, it worsened the situation drastically.

Shortly after the logging boom, residents looked to agriculture as an alternative mean to earn a living, which resulted in removing even more trees. Farmers eliminated existing trees to grow crops, build structures, and heat their homes. Due to deforestation, Door County currently consists of 44 percent farm land and only 37 percent forests. In contrast, the county was originally comprised of one vast forest covering the entire peninsula. Advocates of farming argue that since Door County is known for agriculture, it is necessary to remove trees for the purpose of providing crops. In contrast, Ines Marjanovic, an agronomy expert, contends that it is more important for farmers to increase the yield on existing land and decrease their dependence on deforestation, which would result in producing sufficient crops to feed the growing population. She encourages farmers to utilize more efficient farming practices which include proper tillage, soil analysis, crop rotation, irrigation, and nutrient management. The end result of Marjanovic's analysis is to preserve forests while increasing the yield of existing tillable farm property.

Presently, many forests remain protected by the Door County Land Trust, also known as the DCLT, which was formed in 1986. This organization uses many different methods to preserve land. People can help conserve land by agreeing to have their property placed into a conservation easement. These agreements have helped Door County's landowners protect 3,200 acres of land, with more being added each day. Prior to these agreements, individuals could do with their property as they wished, but the conservation easement restricts them from certain activities which destroy the scenic and ecological purity of the land. The DCLT may limit a landowner's use of property, which poses potential negative consequences including building new residences, installing communication towers and billboards, and clearing forests. The conditional use of donated land would have prevented the prior shipment of 716,400 feet of lumber in Bailey's Harbor alone, which was approximately nine square miles of trees.

Another way people are able to participate in land protection is by donating their property to the DCLT. Land donations are permanent means by which to preserve property and remain binding on future generations of the donor. People can donate land by completing a simple transaction form with the assistance of the DCLT. Members assist landowners in preparing title work, arranging for land surveys, and helping to make necessary decisions on land use.

The Door County Land Trust also retains the option to preserve forests by purchasing property which is ecologically significant and possesses outstanding scenic views. In order for the DCLT to buy land, the property must contain endangered species or a unique tree variety. The view from these forests are usually amazing and include a variety of different animal species and extraordinary, mature plant life. According to Jens Jensen, who is the founder of The Clearing Folk School, "Conservation must not fail, for too much of [the] native landscape has already been thoughtlessly destroyed. Far too much has already been taken by [people] from those who are to follow. It is [people's] sacred duty to preserve what is left for unborn generations." Based on Mr. Jensen's advice, society should learn from past mistakes and preserve the native forests for the enjoyment of future generations. In summary, the objectives of the Door County Land Trust can be achieved by land donations, purchasing unique property, and entering into conservation easement agreements.

The negative consequences of deforestation in Door County, which originated in the 1860s, are avoidable with the guidance of the DCLT. Historical misuse of forests have taught us that excessive logging results in the permanent loss of plant and animal life. Once those resources were diminished, the logging industry left the area or its employees found alternative means to earn a living. Those who stayed in the area and pursued farming realized that there were a number of ways to increase the yield of their tillable land without eliminating trees on their property. The various options presented by the DCLT have protected our spectacular county. The Cathedral of Pines forest, Whitefish Dunes National Park, and Ellison Bluff County Park are making a comeback and providing a great habitat for a wide variety of species.

The success of the Door County Land Trust is obvious to anyone who simply travels through its numerous county parks and along the coasts of

Lake Michigan or Green Bay. The natural beauty of the peninsula has been preserved for residents and vacationers from all over the nation. Door County possesses very unique ecological features and if we are careful in protecting our native forests, there will be no need to imagine a Door County without blossoming cherry trees, chirping birds, and bright fall colors. As residents of Door County, we are entrusted with the obligation and responsibility to preserve our abundant forests for our own enjoyment and the enjoyment of future generations.

Human Health and the Environment

Quality Over Quantity

Written by Erin Tadych

Auliq Ice once stated,
"You'll earn more money doing something you love,
Rather than just doing something because it pays
you a higher salary."
So tell me, farmers, have you lost your passion for
quality dairy products
Because you're afraid you'll suffer economically?
Inconsiderate you remain,

Refusing to look out the window, to see the effects
your selfishness created.

Sitting idle, our Food and Drug Administration
must be naive, or simply doesn't care
About our people's health in relation to increased
antibiotic resistance.
When penicillin and amoxicillin end up in our
meat, soil, and milk,
They'll be the ones to blame for allowing the use of
this venomous chemical in the
First place.
Perhaps the FDA doesn't know the detrimental
effects rBGH has on cattle:
Greater instances of disease and disorders along
with living shorter lives.

The Monsanto Corporation, under the trade name
"Posilac"
Not only produces and sells many poisons, but has
close ties with the FDA—
Strongly shaping the choices of our nation's
organizations.
Weasels and foxes, they mangled their way into
businesses not their own,
And triumphantly succeeded in persuading the
"pros" of their poison;
When the government investigated, no further
action was taken.

Recombinant Bovine Growth Hormone (rBGH) is
produced by genetic engineering.
It duplicates a cow's natural growth hormone,
except rBGH increases milk production—
Five to fifteen percent more than a cow's natural
levels.
rBGH holds no nutritional benefit to consumers, so
why use it?
Labels for rBGH are not required by the FDA:
become informed, shop smart, shop organic.
Grocery bills are cheaper than medical bills.

In Door County, Wisconsin, Renard's Cheese is
rBGH free
Because they know how harmful and unnatural
such a venom can be.
Ann Renard from Renard's Cheese states,
"We pride ourselves in our product being natural.
rBGH is not naturally occurring in the cow and
therefore we disagree with the use.
We find it to be cruel to the animal and a potential
health risk to the consumer."

Quality may be degraded due to rBGH.
Infected udders and an innumerable somatic cell
count causes no good
When bacteria contaminates and spoils milk.
Elevated levels of insulin are a potential threat, so
why take the risk?

Under current investigation, it's suggested Growth
Factor 1 causes tumor growth
In both humans and cows.
Make the right choices to protect your body.

When the chemical first came out, there was no
shortage of cows nor milk.
The purpose? Oh, right—the money.
Yet prices decreased with overproduction.
Organizations like Monsanto and the FDA are
developing a bad reputation
Thanks to farmer's greed and poor decisions.
Why don't these companies and farmers love us as
much as they do money?
Where did the passion for quality over quantity
disappear to?

Genetically Modified Organisms

Written by Maggie Grota

Residents of Door County see and eat GMOs every day, but many people are not aware of the dangerous issues that may arise as a result. GMOs, or genetically modified organisms, contribute to many large problems including chemical spraying, disrupted ecosystems, and unhealthy foods for human consumption. There are many ways in which citizens are able to take a stand against GMOs, but first they must understand the dangerous effects of GMOs on the environment of Door County and their own bodies.

GMOs are often overlooked, but this can be prevented if the public becomes more educated about them. GMOs are any organism altered from their original genetic state including plants, animals, and bacteria. Some common genetically modified products include corn, apples, soy, and sugar beets. According to the USDA, in 2015 the total percentage of GMO corn planted in Wisconsin was a staggering 92 percent. Furthermore, 93 percent of soybeans planted were genetically modified. Crops such as corn and alfalfa, commonly used in animal feed are also genetically modified, meaning that animal products such as milk, cheese, and meat also contain GMOs.

GMO seeds are altered to produce pesticide resistant products, and to yield larger and more numerous crops. The latter, however, proves less valid than some may think. According to the Non GMO Project, "Despite biotech industry promises, there is no evidence that any of the GMOs currently on the market offer increased yield, drought tolerance, enhanced nutrition, or any other consumer benefit." An example of a new GMO is the Arctic® Apple, which contains a genetically engineered trait preventing the apples from browning when exposed to air. According to the Door County Environmental Council's newsletter in Spring of 2013, "[...] the new GMO Arctic® Apple will be drenched in toxic pesticide residues, untested by the U.S. Food & Drug Association (FDA) and likely unlabeled."

GMOs can affect the environment in very powerful ways. One of the most common and most toxic effects of GMOs is the targeted use of specific pesticides and chemicals designed to work with modified crops. Because GMO crops are resistant to these specific pesticides, farmers can spray crops with different chemicals to kill pests. Unfortunately, these chemicals kill other plants and animals not important to the farmers, thus disrupting the ecosystem. One group suffering in particular is the pollinators. The death of honeybees in Door County, as well as the rest of Wisconsin, has escalated dramatically in recent years, mainly due to the increasing amount of pesticides used on GMO crops. According to an article written by Liz Welter in the Green Bay Press Gazette, from 2012 to 2013, the honey bee population in the U.S. has decreased by over fifty percent. The depletion of honey bees in Door County could lead to the loss of crops vital to our economy. Welter explains, "[...] crop losses due to declining pollinators projected by the department include seventy-five percent loss for Wisconsin cranberry growers and an eighty percent loss for apple growers." The use of chemicals can also result in superbugs and superweeds—insects and weeds tolerant to pesticides. Because of this, stronger chemicals such as 2,4- D, a toxic chemical found in Agent Orange (a herbicide used for warfare during the Vietnam War from which victims suffered serious health issues), are applied, in turn creating stronger and more numerous weeds and insects. According to the Stratus

Agriculture Research company, "In a survey of US farmers, nearly half (49 percent) said they had Roundup-resistant (glyphosate-resistant) weeds on their farm in 2012, up from 34 percent of farmers in 2011." To date, there have been no major cases of superbugs in Door County. However, if GMO crops are continuously planted and soaked in toxic chemicals, it is almost certain that superbugs will become an issue.

GMOs also pose potential threats to the human body. Because GMOs are a relatively new phenomenon, substantial studies have not yet been performed to provide an accurate view of the direct effects of GMOs on human health. It is known, however, that chemicals commonly sprayed on GMOs can cause harm to the body. The International Agency for Research for Cancer (IARC) classified Glyphosate as a probable human carcinogen, and 2,4-D as a possible carcinogen.

We, the citizens of Door County, must take a stand against the use of GMOs in our county. One of the most effective ways that residents can accomplish this is through buying from local, organic, non-GMO farms such as Wildwood, Steep Creek, and Waseda farms. Although their products may cost a dollar or two more, you will support the environment, your health, and the local economy. When addressing why residents should eat and buy organic, organic farmer Linda Cockburn (Owner of Sunner Farm in West Jacksonport Door County), stated "It's true food. It's food that tastes the way you remember it tasting—before it became leached of its flavor and nutrients. But most importantly, every effort and every dollar spent on organic products is a vote for the sustainability of our world." Door County residents or visitors may also visit local farmers markets across the county which provide local and organic foods and products. One other way you can fight against GMOs is by planting a garden. Citizens can either grow a garden at their own homes, or rent out a garden plot at the Community Garden in Sturgeon Bay for forty dollars per year. This is a wonderful opportunity for local citizens to assist and educate their community on the use of fresh, organic foods.

GMOs threaten the wonderful environment that Door County residents are fortunate to enjoy. Citizens possess the ability to create change within a community though their decisions and actions. Every step, big or small, proves to be a step in the right direction. Deeming GMOs an issue of the past is achievable if the citizenry is properly educated, resulting in a healthier and happier Door County with a thriving ecosystem.

Mortified

Written by Erin Tadych

Darting and dancing,
Invading, infecting
Undetected chemicals remain

One by one, leaves fall
Brown and fragile
As bark flakes from its body
Shriveled trees,
Desperate to survive the assault
From insalubrious substances

Attacked with sickness,
Infestation, evil
Demise creeps in

Potent chemicals release havoc
On the human foundation
Down one lung then the other
Liver, glands, and heart
From necrosis to the ultimate death
Ending all functions

Vile and impure
Wicked and corrupt
It's still not seen

The sweet melodic tune birds sing
Disappears
And the brilliant buzz from bees
Gone
From blissfully beautiful to barren
Nature crumbles in humanity's hands

Why act so selfishly
By turning a blind eye
To our collapse?

Our constellations are masked
By their synthetic brother
In Chicago, New York, Los Angeles
And someday, the biggest star of all

Might be clouded by our chemicals

Swimming and falling
Acid rain
Washing away life

A drop of water alters the flow
Colors change with chemicals
Seeping, contaminating the clear
A ripple effect

Harmful Habits, Sinful Cycle

Written by Shaina Skaletski

Many people would agree their environment impacts them. Such informed individuals would stress an inviting space causes them to be more socially interactive and improves their mood. They would also stress that since nature is capable of affecting them positively, it has the ability to affect them negatively. The physical wellbeing of Door County citizens is threatened by the harsh effects that come with Door County's surplus of water contaminants and carbon emissions.

To expand on the harm caused by water contaminants, multitudes of health risks are induced by the consumption of waste in groundwater. Hepatitis, dysentery, and poisoning exist as the most detrimental health problems. Hepatitis types A and E are caused when contaminated water enters the digestive system, in some cases causing irreversible damage. Also brought about by consuming polluted water is the more common intestinal infection, dysentery. Symptoms of dysentery include vomiting, bloody stool, fever, and fatal dehydration lasting up to a week. Door County citizens should be more cautious of this issue than citizens of other counties due to Door County's increased susceptibility to water pollution.

The Wisconsin Department of Natural Resources found Door County's bedrock is at the shallow depth of zero to five feet deep, consisting mostly of carbonate type rock. The soil, in addition to the bedrock, is highly permeable and has low filtration of destructive substances. Residents of Door County are further inclined to the health issues brought with water contamination considering seventy percent of Wisconsin's population and 97 percent of Wisconsin communities rely on groundwater as their drinking source.

Also negatively impacting the health of Door County citizens is climate change. Climate change is prevalent in Door County due to the Lake Michigan coasts baring a warmer, wetter climate. This increase in temperature can lead to serious health risks that many citizens are not aware of such as the development of allergies, asthma, cancer, and other threatening illnesses. Rebecca Leber of *New Republic* states, "Climate change lengthens allergy season and raises pollen counts. An increase in ozone and carbon pollution contributes to pollen counts, while extreme rainfall and dampness encourages the growth of indoor fungi and molds." This is proved with the statistic, "Between 1995 and 2011, hotter temperatures caused the ragweed pollen season to increase by anywhere from 11 to 27 days in parts of the U.S." The Center for Health and the Global Environment at Harvard Medical School reinforces this statement by adding, "As global temperature rises, diseases that were previously found only in warmer areas of the world are showing up increasingly in other, previously cooler areas, where people have not yet developed natural defenses against them." With Door County being a "previously cooler area," its people, by the terms previously stated, are more susceptible to the health risks brought with increased temperature. Asthma, allergies, diseases, and food illnesses are also a consequence of the change in weather patterns. The increased heat has created a perfect environment for bacteria like salmonella, cholera, and more to contaminate our food and water.

It is vital for the people of Door County to reduce their carbon emissions and eliminate water waste because, if ignored, these issues could damage their physical well-being. There are many steps you can take to address the expressed environmental issues, ultimately decreasing the risk of contracting these illnesses. For example, you can reduce your carbon releases by investing in renewable energy sources which generate energy without emitting carbon into the atmosphere. By utilizing public transportation as well as biking and walking, people help reduce exhaust emissions. In 2015 the U.S. Environmental Protection Agency found that transportation accounted for 27 percent of America's greenhouse gas emissions. Simple transportation choices significantly impact the air we breathe.

As for eliminating the waste found in Door County's groundwater, managing waste and using fewer, less harmful chemicals will improve water quality. This is achieved by properly disposing potentially toxic substances, such as pharmaceuticals and paint, and using natural, nontoxic products. Reinitiating The Door County Household Hazardous Collection Event, which invites all residents to "rid their households of unwanted wastes for free," may encourage the community at large to partake.

Now we must ask ourselves the question asked by *Scientific American:* "Will people care more about the environment with a better understanding of how it affects them personally?"

65

Natural vs. Synthetic

Written by Alex Quigley

Have you ever walked around in a grocery store and noticed the organic foods section, or perhaps a variety of natural remedies? Many people have already made the switch from synthetic to natural products, but is there scientific research to back this up? The benefits of natural products outweigh those of synthetics because they don't pose as many threats to humanity.

By definition, natural products come straight from nature with no modifications whatsoever. Synthetic products are defined as "a substance

made by chemical synthesis, especially to imitate a
natural product." In Door County, all-natural and
organic food selections are very common. More and
more restaurants are making the switch to organic
natural foods because the food they originally used
didn't have as much flavor and was of lower quality.
Natural food has more flavor because nothing
within it has been synthetically modified. Some of
the food that restaurants (such as The Bluefront
Cafe, The Get "Real" Cafe, and Chives) received was
injected with antibiotics and hormones, leading to
the dilution of flavor in the food. Processing food
can also hurt the essential flavor of the food. Food
processing typically involves activities such as
mincing, liquefying, cooking (via boiling, frying,
broiling, and/or grilling), pickling, pasteurization,
canning, and many other preserving methods, along
with packaging. Some other common practices are
slicing, dicing, freezing, and drying. These
processes can result in a loss of flavor and
nutritional value.

Another commonality in Door County is the
usage of natural products for medicinal purposes.
People talk about using natural products such as
echinacea, essential oils, fish oils, and CBD.
Benefits of using natural products include no side
effects, no risk of overdose, and no addiction. In
addition, many of these products are cheaper and
are jam-packed with antioxidants. When synthetic
forms of medications are made, they are identical to

the natural version, except for a few alterations. These changes can result in side effects and addictive properties. In contrast, essential oils have none of these. It's impossible to become addicted to essential oils. Everyone knows of people that have become addicted to drugs; it's inevitable in today's culture. But does it have to be? The switch from synthetic to natural drugs can help reduce prescription drug abuse. One of the best parts about natural medicines is that they are actually cheaper than the synthetic versions. DoTERRA is one of the world's largest essential oil companies and is also a third-party tested source. Third party testing entails sending their products to other companies for it to be tested, ensuring the safety of the products. Based on studies from DoTERRA and their third party sources, natural compounds are cheaper than over-the-counter medications and actually work faster as shown below.

Essential Oils vs. Traditional Medicine			
Ailment	Treatment	Cost	Time
Child's Fever	Peppermint Oil	7 ¢	2 – 3 min.
	Fever Medication	50 ¢	30+ min.
Upset Stomach	DigestZen Oil	12 ¢	seconds
	Over the Counter Medication	70 ¢	15 - 30 min.
Ear Infection	Lavender & Melaleuca Oils	25 ¢	1 day
	Doctor visit & Antibiotics	$50+	7 - 10 days

One of the last reasons to switch to natural medications is antioxidants. Antioxidants are substances that can prevent or delay types of cell damage. They are found in many foods, including fruits and vegetables, and also many natural medicines. Vegetables, fruits, and other plants are rich sources of antioxidants; in fact, clover is one of the richest sources of antioxidants known on the face of the Earth, followed by blueberries. There is evidence that eating a diet with a variety of fruits and vegetables lowers risk of certain diseases and prevents aging due to the antioxidants found within them. Although there are synthetic, dietary supplements of antioxidants on the market, people are much better off buying fruits and vegetables.

Natural products are also available in beauty products, pesticides, repellents, and cleaning supplies. Beauty products are a staple in the American lifestyle, including facial primers, concealers and foundations, all different types of powders, eye makeup, lipsticks, and facial cleansing masks. All of which have safer, healthier, natural alternatives. Many beauty products cause skin irritations and breakouts. In 2010, an organization by the name of COSMOS was created, in order to create an international standard for organic cosmetics. "Beauty is a global industry," says The Soil Association, which along with four other organizations recognizes COSMOS as a worldwide standard. Since the 1st of January 2017, all newly certified products with the COSMOS label have met the COSMOS standards, which will eventually become the mainstream global standards for organic health and beauty.

In the past, The Soil Association encouraged huge corporations to increase the quality of their packaging so that synthetic cosmetic products wouldn't get into the soil around the world. With the huge transition to natural/organic cosmetics, those environmental concerns are solved, and people can still look just as good as before. The switch would also be an easy transition into Door County lifestyles, for these COSMOS approved products are already in stores.

Pesticides and insect repellents are also major threats to Door County's ecosystem. Natural pesticides and insect repellents are on the market and are better for the environment in most cases. Insect repellents can be made using all natural products like lemongrass. In most countries, insect repellents come in aerosol cans containing chlorofluorocarbons, which have a dramatic effect on the ozone layer. Chlorofluorocarbons are very reactive with the chemical structure found in ozone, one of the many reasons there are such huge holes. Scientists have concluded that aerosol cans containing things like chlorofluorocarbons are a large contributor to the "holes" in the ozone, according to *Scientific American*. There are ways to completely avoid using aerosols such as spray bottles with lemongrass water or the use of essential oils diluted in water.

Household cleaners are found in every home across America, but the question remains how safe they are. Chemical cleaners are extremely unsafe properties to begin with, but with children around, they can be life threatening. It is common knowledge that Clorox Bleach is an extremely unsafe chemical, yet it is found in almost every home in the US. *Educating Wellness* states, "The dangers of bleach and other cleaning products are well documented but many times 'brushed under the rug' for profit." Throughout U.S. history, the U.S. government has allowed for unsafe, toxic products to get into the hands of the U.S. citizen so that big corporations can make huge profits. The book *Silent Spring* exposed how the U.S. government has allowed and even paid big corporations to do full scale sprayings across the country using dangerous chemicals like DDT, which detrimentally affected the U.S. wildlife. So who is to trust when buying products? It has been shown that the government doesn't do anything to control big business. Instead of giving in to big corporations, people can make their own cleaning supplies, naturally. Citrus fruits have a compound within them that has effects similar to those of bleach, but without all the dangerous effects. According to *Modern Essentials*, it has been scientifically proven that citrus fruits are a safe, natural alternative to toxic cleaning supplies sold in stores across America.

In conclusion, it's very simple and beneficial to go natural. Natural products are the best way to go and have been from the very beginning. The next time you are at the grocery store, take some time to go down the natural and organic aisle. You may find it to be one of the best decisions in your life.

Zero Waste: Eliminating–Not Minimizing–the Problem

Written by Helen Parks

The average American produces about four pounds of trash per day, most of which is sent to sit in a landfill and release toxic gases and chemicals into the atmosphere, creating health problems. These unnatural chemicals are also seeping into the soil and groundwater, contaminating it. The steady increase in waste has created more landfills which, in turn, create more problems.

The abundance of garbage and trash in our country and community creates more health problems as we produce more waste. According to the New York Department of Health, small periods of exposure to large amounts of ammonia and hydrogen sulfide in the air causes coughing; irritation of the eyes, nose, and throat; headaches; nausea; and breathing difficulties. Studies have been conducted by communities to evaluate the health effects associated with exposure to gases produced by nearby landfills. The studies, conducted over several months, reported health complaints including eye, throat, and lung irritation; nausea; headaches; nasal blockage; sleeping difficulties; weight loss; chest pain; and aggravation of asthma.

Another danger produced by landfills is leachate. Leachate is water that has been filtered through a solid and contains some of the components of the solid. Landfills everywhere are unknowingly producing leachate that is draining into the soil and water in the surrounding environment. Trichloroethylene (TCE) is a carcinogen typically found in landfill leachate. TCE is a man-made chlorinated solvent used commercially for industrial degreasers, spot removers, and dry cleaning. Drinking or inhaling TCE can lead to damage of the liver, kidneys, central nervous system, and also increases the risk of cancer. Less than four drops of TCE mixed with the water in an average swimming pool would contaminate the water and leave it undrinkable. Eighty-two percent of landfills today have leaks within the liners and forty-one percent have a leak area over one square foot. The U.S. Environmental

Protection Agency has stated that, even with double liners, the probability of leaking is still very high and estimates that between one tenth of a percent and four tenths of a percent of usable surface aquifers are contaminated by landfills, according to WeGreen-USA.

A solution to many of the problems associated with landfills is a zero waste lifestyle. A zero waste lifestyle is exactly what it sounds like: no waste. The definition of a person who is a "zero waster" is a person who tries to send nothing to a landfill. They reduce and reuse as much as they can, send as little as possible to be recycled, and compost their remaining waste. What does zero waste do for the environment? "Zero Waste means designing and managing products and processes to systematically avoid and eliminate the volume and toxicity of waste and materials, conserve and recover all resources, and not burn or bury them. Implementing Zero Waste will eliminate all discharges to land, water, or air that are a threat to planetary, human, animal or plant health." Zero waste living aims to eliminate rather than minimize the waste problem.

By using and buying less waste, we not only reduce the amount of waste we produce but improve our everyday health. Most "zero wasters" buy their food from farmers' markets, bulk stores, or grow it themselves. This means that all their food is all natural and in its original raw state. Eating healthy unprocessed foods can lead to living a more healthy lifestyle rather than eating foods with ingredients most people can't pronounce.

Another way that living a zero waste lifestyle can improve your everyday health is by using all natural cosmetics and toiletries. You can use baking soda as deodorant to replace the nasty chemicals used in everyday health and beauty routines. Instead of using makeup wipes to clean your face, use a washcloth and soap because the washcloth can be washed and reused. Many people think that they would be unable to wear makeup because of the containers it is kept in, but there are many different natural recipes you can use to make your own makeup. Men and women can purchase metal shavers online that come with recyclable razor blades and can use shaving soap or coconut oil in place of shaving cream. The list can go on and on. With careful thought and research anyone can transform their everyday morning routine to zero waste.

When you live a zero waste lifestyle, you reduce the harmful effects that plastic has on the environment as well. Plastic may seem the everyday superhero, helping to make our lives easier, but it has turned out to be a very harmful substance. Chemicals added to plastics can be absorbed by the human body, which may lead to alterations in hormones and other potential health dangers. Additionally, plastic problems affect more than just humans; they extend to the animals in our environment. Over one hundred eighty species of animals ingest plastic debris, including birds, fish, turtles and marine mammals. Phthalates are a group of chemicals used to soften and increase the flexibility of plastic and vinyl. Bisphenol A (BPA) is an industrial chemical that has been used to make certain plastics and resins. A laboratory study showed that phthalates and BPA's affect reproduction in all studied animal groups and impairs the development in crustaceans and amphibians. By avoiding plastic and utilizing reusable products in your everyday life, you can help to reduce the amount of plastic produced and discarded around the country and world.

In 2005, Eco-Cycle launched the Green Stars Schools program in four pilot elementary schools located in Boulder County, Colorado. Their goal was to transition the schools to becoming zero waste. They were able to reduce their waste by two thirds as a result of increasing recycling of paper product and commingled containers, composting food waste from their kitchens and cafeterias, and training staff and students on environmental education. In 2012, Green Bay city council members thought that a trash-to-energy incinerator was needed to reduce the amount of trash going into landfills. They began to promote the idea of zero waste, but the Green Bay city council vetoed the permit for the construction of an incinerator. If you don't have room to compost your yard waste like lawn clippings, leaves, and garden waste, Sturgeon Bay offers a compost site for all residents within the city limits. Anyone can then contact the compost site about purchasing compost. This reduces the amount of yard waste that is sent to landfills and dumps and helps to boost the environment by promoting compost production.

Door County has thin and poor soil resulting in the need to transport most of our garbage to sites in nearby counties. Door County's only landfill is on Washington Island, which is due to there being no easy way to transport waste off the island. Our water is very susceptible to contamination, and a small amount of garbage sitting for a while could contaminate it. Having a large landfill on a small island surrounded by a great lake doesn't sound like a good combination. Although it may not be a large problem in Door County today, it could become one soon with our massive output of trash needing space to be stored. If Door County does develop a landfill in the near future, the chances of water and soil pollution are very high, so adapting a zero waste lifestyle can help to reduce the future need of a landfill.

You may think one person can only make a small dent in a huge problem, but every solution has to start somewhere. Instead of using plastic bags at the grocery store, bring cloth reusable bags. You can buy food from bulk stores depending on where you live. Purchase foods packaged in metal or paper, not plastic. Use reusable containers for your lunch and try to compost any table scraps or leftovers you don't eat. These are just a few examples of small things we can do in our everyday life that can make a big change in your community.

When you live a zero waste lifestyle, you are showing that you care about the community you live in and the environment you are going to leave for future generations. Living a zero waste lifestyle not only benefits the environment we live in, but our general health, too. If everyone lived a semi-wasteless lifestyle, it would help to eliminate the problem rather than just minimizing it. Taking a small part in fixing a big problem might help to one day eliminate the problem altogether.

Invasive Species

Aquatic Hitchhikers

Written by Eli Jeanquart

    Invasive species loom over us like a threatening shadow, putting our natural wildlife at risk. These organisms run rampant because of the lack of natural predators, inevitably destroying the complex relationships between the native species. Overall, we need to be aware of what invasive species are, what they do, and how to control and prevent them.

    The sea lamprey, an eel-like fish, is an organism that attaches itself to other fish. Identified in the mid-1800s, they slowly made their way into Lake Michigan. Sea lampreys that live in the Great

Lakes consume up to forty pounds of fish throughout their 12-18 month feeding period. As a result, the local fishing industry suffered. The amount of trout, a prime prey for the sea lamprey, decreased to about ten percent of the original 1,800 tons when sea lamprey were first introduced. The Great Lakes Fishery Commission estimated that the overall annual catch in the Great Lakes dropped from a hefty 15 million pounds to only three hundred thousand pounds, 2 percent of the original amount.

Because of the overabundance and immediate threat of sea lampreys, the Wisconsin DNR generated methods to control them so they couldn't spread and cause more damage. The first attempt at removal was placing electrified barriers in streams where the sea lamprey were known to spawn. This proved ineffective in decreasing the sea lamprey population and caused many problems. The barriers wouldn't incapacitate all of the adult sea lampreys unless an extremely high voltage was used. This wouldn't just kill sea lamprey, but all the fish that used the stream as well. The second treatment used was a chemical called TFM, which targeted the ammocoete stage of the sea lamprey. This treatment proved effective, decreasing the population by 86 percent, but adverse effects towards the other species in the area surfaced. This treatment is gradually being phased out due to increasing cost of the chemical and observed negative effects to other wildlife. Another method utilized is the sea lamprey sterile male program. This releases twenty thousand sterile males into the waters, effectively "tricking" the sea lamprey into assuming their eggs have been fertilized.

An additional species invading our waters is the zebra mussel. Native to Russia and Ukraine, these mussels arrived in Lake Michigan in the early 1990s and quickly became a potent threat. The mussels hurt many aspects of our life, including our economy and environment. Due to their lack of predators in the Great Lakes, they spread uncontrollably, consuming all food in the region and thereby starving the native species to the brink of extinction.

Zebra mussels are also thought to be a source of avian botulism (a paralytic disease caused by ingestion of a toxin produced by the *Clostridium botulinum* bacteria), which has claimed the lives of roughly ten thousand birds since their introduction. As zebra mussels filter water through their gills, they accumulate deadly toxins and pollutants in their tissues which can pass through the food chain, eventually reaching humans, as their typical predators are smallmouth bass and crayfish.

Another effect of their water filtration abilities includes the surrounding water becoming clearer. While this may seem beneficial, it invokes fatal consequences on the local aquatic environment. The clearer the water, the deeper the sun's rays penetrate, eventually reaching weeds rooted to the lake floor and increasing their growth rate. Ironically, as they grow and reach the surface, they effectively block out the sun and alter the aquatic ecosystem. This leads to decreased rate of growth for other important plants and decreased amount of accessible food for larger fish.

Zebra mussels also profoundly affect the economy. Control and prevention for zebra mussels alone costs about five hundred thousand dollars per year in addition to approximately $250,000 for electricity and water treatment facilities. Also, zebra mussels have a habit of attaching themselves to, and sometimes damaging, intake pipes and municipal water supplies, which can impede water flow.

In brief, if we wait until these species have infested our ecosystem, there might not be anything left to save. To preserve what we value, we must change how invasive species are managed and observed in Door County. Not only do government officials need to change but we, the people of Door County, need to change as well. We can prevent more invasives from entering and spreading throughout our environment by making sure our vehicles are clean of aquatic hitchhikers, preventing the movement of infested vessels, and many other ways. If nothing is done about these intruders, Door County will surely succumb to the influence of invasive species.

Insignificant Moths; Monumental Issues

Written by Zoey Kohler

We toss our empty coke bottles out the window as we cruise down Highway 57, hiding insecurities behind Ray Banz and throwing caution to the wind while momentarily ignoring our environmental responsibilities. We may feel that this single action won't impact the fate of the Earth, but before assuming our insignificance, let's delve into the story of Ginny the Gypsy Moth.

Seemingly humble and infinitesimal, the gypsy moth starts out as a larva who shares a small egg mass home with her brothers and sisters before emerging in early spring. Many of the larvae, tiny in size and mass, suspend themselves in the crisp air by silky threads. The wind carries some larvae miles away, while other larvae hitch rides on vehicles and people to new places.

Ginny has another plan in mind. She heads straight to the great oak's foliage to munch. She spends her days slinking about and devouring leaf after leaf. The larvae mingle around the top of the tree at night but hide away when the sun comes out to play. They eat; they molt; they grow. Escaping birds and beetles is their only worry.

That is, until the great oak tree's branches are stripped of leaves. Ginny and her accomplices abandon the crime scene and travel through the jungle of grass and rumblings of footsteps to the next victim: a basswood. Then on to the next tree, and the next. They gorge; they spread; they destroy. Soon the decreased leafage struggles to sustain the trees, but the larvae ravish on.

Once plump in preparation for pupation, Ginny hunkers down under a fallen branch. She has done her damage and will carry on the tradition. When she emerges a moth, she mates and lays the eggs that will develop into next year's lethal larvae. The cycle repeats year after year, causing the branches to grow narrower and the foliage more sparse.

The meager gypsy larva impacts the Earth simply by eating and reproducing. One moth lays approximately 1,000 eggs. Each egg grows to eat more than a square yard of leaves. Gypsy moths have collectively defoliated millions of acres of trees. With each impacted tree, the decreased forestry uproots countless animals' livelihoods, and the gypsy moths' ecological effects are spreading westward across the United States. Nature's balance lies within each species, no matter the size.

We blame the moths, but we created this problem. The gypsy moths, *Lymantria dispar*, first appeared in the United States due to a mistake by a young French entomologist named Etienne Trouvelot. While attempting to breed them with silk worms, some moths escaped and have dispersed across the country.

Efforts to control the moths with fungi, sticky tapes, and predator species are underway. Nevertheless, the best treatments are preventative measures, as this mistake could have been avoided. We may have to manage the aftermath of this disaster, but other incidences developing right under our noses demand our attention.

Our environment is changing on our account. We witness the impact of the tiny gypsy moth but somehow continue to feel we have no power. Perhaps these feelings of insignificance originate in our insecurities, in which case, we must be brave. Before throwing garbage on the ground because "one time won't make a difference," remember the story of the gypsy moth. Every action creates repercussions, good or bad. Please, recycle your coke bottle. Stand tall and spread the word that we leave a mark on our world. We have an impact; let's make it a good one.

The Cancer of Our Ash Trees

Written by Grace LeGrave

Emerald Ash Borers, otherwise known as EABs, have significantly impacted Door County's ash trees in recent years, and the problem is going to worsen if we don't put a stop to it. In order to do this, we need to prevent this invasive insect from spreading and eventually killing all of our ash trees. They are a cancer, a phenomenon perceived to be destructive and hard to contain or eradicate, and need to be stopped. Our ecosystems are in danger, and with no natural predators, the problem might soon be uncontainable. We need to be aware of occurrences, effects, and prevention of the Emerald Ash Borer to keep Door County as safe and healthy as it can be.

The discoveries of Emerald Ash Borer infestations are rising. This native species of Asia was transported to America through wood packing materials in 2002 and has now reached Wisconsin. Door County has become the 22nd county where the invasive beetle has been found. The first occurrences of this harmful insect in Door County were in 2014 near Fish Creek and Sturgeon Bay. Since then, they have been spreading throughout more state, county, and city land. Bill Ruff, a forester with the DNR, states, "We've reached the point now where we have almost half the townships in the county [with] confirmed locations with the ash borer, so the spread is on." Along with Sturgeon Bay and Fish Creek, other known locations of the EAB are on Washington and Rock Island. Before we know it, every city will be infected and our county will no longer have the ash trees that are necessary for our environment. Earlier this year, over 25 ash trees were removed within Sturgeon Bay due to infestation, and the numbers are still rising. Door County's ash trees make up more than 12 percent of the 115 million trees in our county. That is more than 12 million trees! Some kind of action needs to be taken to preserve these beautiful trees.

89

There are many signs that reveal if an ash tree is being affected by EABs. The start of damage begins when adult beetles lay their eggs on the top of the bark. Then, the larvae burrow beneath the bark and block the flow of nutrients by feeding on transportation tissues, eventually killing it. Therefore, one of the most important steps to preserve the ash trees is early detection. This allows for the tree to be treated and possibly saved if detected early enough. However, if you notice things such as dead leaves on the top of the tree, D-shaped holes, falling bark, and woodpeckers eating the bugs, it might be too late to save the tree. On their own, EABs travel very slowly, only about a mile every year. However, human transportation of wood to uninfested areas greatly increases this rate. Therefore, it's always important to be cautious while transporting wood and to always be on the watch for the effects of EAB. Todd Burke, a certified arborist with Dave's Tree Service of Egg Harbor, states, "When you think about it, if there are 12 million ash trees and in six to seven years they are going to be dead, that impact in Door County will be huge."

We cannot afford to lose our ash trees. They provide a sort of canopy for plants, animals, and even humans. Plants and animals that have adapted to the shade under ashes are now suddenly exposed to the sunlight and have to find a way to recover. Also, humans make use of the ash trees during everyday life. They provide us shade and are common among many neighborhoods.

Preventing EAB in the county will protect the ash trees and make for a healthier environment. As stated before, one of the most important steps to protect the ash trees is early detection. Some people may resort to using the simple solution to defend against EAB: insecticides. However, these harmful chemicals cost a lot of money, take years of treatment, and will lead to more environmental problems. It is not reasonable to treat millions of trees. Property owners with one or two ash trees can treat the trees in order to limit damage from beetles, but owners of many ash trees might have a tougher time. On June 3rd, 2017 an Ash Borer management workshop was held in New London, WI to inform the public how to control the EAB. If we continue workshops like these to teach how to spot the signs and protect our trees, then we will take more progressive steps to containing the insect.

Many citizens are aware of the regulation of firewood. This quarantine prohibits the movement of ash wood to non-quarantined counties so EAB is not transmitted. This mostly concerns campgrounds where EAB might be common. With Door County having many cabins and campgrounds, it is especially important to follow the regulations. Firewood brought from within 20 miles of a state park campground used to be acceptable, but new standards have reduced this to 10 miles away. Most campgrounds in Door County simply require firewood to be bought and burned on site. This is definitely the best way to handle firewood that can easily be plagued by the beetle.

If we don't start taking action now, the ash trees of Door County will be gone before we know it. This cancer of our ash trees will soon be uncontrollable, taking out each and every ash tree one at a time. We need to stay strong and fight for the health of our environment. We all loathe cancers among our loved ones, so why are we letting this "cancer" continue to take over the ash trees? It is not fair for them to be left defenseless while society simply sits back and watches it happen. Next time you're taking a walk or strolling down the street, look for the signs of EAB infestation. Take action and inform others on how to prevent as well as detect EAB. If the current ways of "fighting" against EAB are improved, it is very possible that we can save the beloved ashes. In order to achieve this, the public needs to be informed on the occurrences, effects, and prevention of EAB.

Population Predicaments

The Legend of the Orchid

Written by Grace Englebert

In the beginning, Door County's native plants and animals lived in perfect harmony. Nature ebbed and flowed for millions of years, cycling through Ice Ages, Green Ages, and everything in between. One day, only a mere 12,000 years ago, strong and healthy Mother Nature encountered the first nomadic peoples on the beautiful peninsula. They immediately recognized their dependence on Mother Nature and quickly developed a close relationship with her. For another ten millennia, Door County was in harmony; however, the eleventh millenia brought with it eminent environmental destruction—Europeans. These people disregarded the health of Mother Nature. They cut down her ancient forests to make room for livestock and crops, depleted her soil of all nutrients, and harvested lumber from her old-growth forests. By the early twentieth century, Mother Nature lay in ruin. While farmers ignored the result of their ignorance, any hope for the restoration of the once plentiful peninsula disappeared.

For years residents scraped by, producing just enough to survive. It could not get any worse, they thought. However, in the year 1934, Mother Nature's health rapidly declined. As her strength faded, a drought of unprecedented severity struck. The Dust Bowl of 1934 brought wicked sand storms from the south, and in desperation, the people called out to Mother Nature. Not receiving any response, they begged and pleaded only to realize that abused and barren, she could no longer provide for them. In complete despair, citizens gave up all hope.

Refusing to idly allow their own actions to cause their demise, a small group of citizens came together to save their beloved peninsula. Over the next three years, Albert Fuller led his comrades in the restoration of 40 acres of land known as The Ridges. While The Ridges only accounted for one hundredth of a percent of Door County's total land area, it was just enough to help Mother Nature begin to heal. To thank the citizens dedicated to saving her, Mother Nature gifted the peninsula the orchid—a flower to indicate her health. If she ever began to deteriorate again, the orchids would die and citizens would have the chance to save her before it was too late.

Grateful for her forgiveness and generosity, citizens began donating land, so by 1970, the sanctuary had swelled to a size of 700 acres and in 2015 it reached 1,600 acres—over five hundredths of a percent of Door County's total land area.

Currently, orchids are endangered not only in Door County, but across the United States. Playing an active role in their restoration, The Ridges Sanctuary endeavours to identify the cause. However, one thing is for sure: the orchids are dying and Mother Nature is soon to follow.

The Honey Bee

Written by Elyse Columb

Most people are unaware of the many positive effects honey bees have for both them and the environment. This species plays an important role in the maintenance of Door County throughout the spring and summer months. It is crucial to protect the bees and grow their population because of their multitude of contributions to the Door County area. These include their pollination benefits, honey production, and economic contributions. However, the honey bee is diminishing in numbers as a result of mites and pesticides. If we continue to let the population decline, the benefits bees give to Door County will disappear.

The first thing honey bees do is improve and assist pollination in Door County. This positive contribution in turn benefits consumers and the economy in numerous ways. The best example of this is cherry trees. A lack of pollination of these fruit trees would cause two main problems. Due to Door County being famous for cherry trees, a decreased number of honey bees would negatively affect our profit and economy because the cherries wouldn't bring in the expected amount of revenue. If there aren't enough bees flying around transferring pollen, the cherry trees won't flourish. A decrease in cherries would result in a decline of tourists because not enough cherries would exist to go around. The other problem would be a money deficit for the people growing and selling the cherries. A decrease in cherry output would cause producers to lose profit, which would lead to less money being put into the economy as a result of choosing to save the money rather than spending it. For example, if a cherry orchard experienced a spring with a low honey bee count, it would cause the trees to yield lower amounts of fruit. To compensate for the loss, the grower would put more in savings and spend less on extra clothes, hobbies, electronics, or other items.

In addition to pollinating the cherry trees, honey bees also help pollinate gardens, which further benefits us in Door County, right in our own backyards. When a healthy bee population is present, gardens create a healthy amount of produce due to how much pollination the bees promote. The more produce there is, the cheaper the foods from the garden become for the consumer. The honey bee pollinates by collecting pollen and then flying to another plant. In this process, the pollen is transferred from plant to plant. Thinking on more of a personal level, wouldn't you want your own personal garden to flourish? Wouldn't you prefer cheaper fruits and vegetables? Having bees present within Door County creates a perfect balance between the demand for produce and the price consumers have to pay for that produce. This is why people need to take action and protect such an important species.

Another positive effect of honey bees is honey, which is the only food made by an insect. Everyone loves a jar of delectable honey, but if the bee population drops, there won't be as much honey to enjoy. Bees produce honey by first collecting nectar from flowers, then mixing it with an enzyme they produce in their mouth. Once this is completed, it is stored in a honeycomb. The honey bees then proceed to speed up evaporation of the water within the honey by flapping their wings over the honeycomb. The last step is to enclose the honey with a layer of wax. Once beekeepers notice the wax on the honeycomb, they know the honey is ready to be harvested. However, if a honey bee colony does not have enough bees within it, they lack the efficiency to make enough honey. Since honey is what the bees eat during winter, it's crucial they have ample amounts. It's also worth noting that a decreased amount of honey will increase the price, so if you love honey, show your support towards the honey bee by donating money or joining a Beekeeper's Club.

Unfortunately, calamitous factors are causing a decline in the bee population. One reason is the use of specific pesticides that weaken and kill the honey bees. Some of these pesticides include neonicotinoids and permethrin. Neonicotinoids harm the bees by contaminating the pollen, which the bees then come in contact with and ingest. Permethrin, on the other hand, is a stomach poison found naturally in *Chrysanthemum* flowers. Some of its intended uses are to treat head lice and control mosquitoes. Unfortunately, both of these chemicals harm more than their target, and the honey bee happens to be one of them. To prevent these chemicals from causing more damage, it is recommended that the pesticides not be directly sprayed onto flowers and any required spraying should take place in the late or night hours. This will limit the harmful effects on bees because they don't forage at night. Another cause of the bees' ruination are mites. The most damaging mite to bee colonies is the Varroa mite. These pests kill bees like vampires, sucking the blood out of them, which results in the weakening of their bodies and death once the winter months arrive. Varroa mites are eight legged and dark brown, making them easy to spot if an infestation is suspected within the colony. Early detection is critical in bee preservation because if left untreated, these mites could wipe out entire colonies.

We the people of Door County can help restore the honey bee population through many endeavors. One of which is to join the Door County Beekeepers Club, an organization that is very welcoming of new members and accepts donations towards the honey bee. This organization came to Door County a couple of years ago when the honey bee population started to plummet. This club is very dedicated to their cause: "Our mission is to promote the study, science and craft of beekeeping through education, encouragement and community for all Door County beekeepers, and raise awareness to the benefits of bees for our environment, ecology and local economy." If you want to channel your creative side, build habitats for the bees to help restore the population. If you'd rather focus on the chemical dangers, reducing pesticide use is an effective way to save this species. This can be done by using more natural alternatives to keep infestations down or not using anything at all, which would let nature work it out by itself. You can also keep yourself informed on the honey bee and their happenings through news articles or other essays, so you know how you can help save such a preeminent species. The bees require the help and support of Door County to thrive; we are the support system the bees desperately need.

No Trees, No Cherries

Written by MaCayla Moore

The Bing Cherry tree is a delicious fruit-bearing topiary essential to the core of our "cherry" county. The cherry industry is far from collapsing, but the will to own and manage a full orchard is becoming scarce. The decline in the trees' health should be a major concern for our community, and with our help it can be nursed back to its former glory. In the small town of Forestville, Wisconsin, an orchard that had been thriving for over a century was destroyed. The leaves had crumbled and the limbs had snapped off. The pits were covered by

103

crispy cherries only weeks after finally ripening to a bright, juicy red. This is not an unusual occurrence, and it is only a taste of the heart-shattering effects of overspraying with dangerous chemicals, extreme weather conditions, and overpowering insects.

One of the most easily preventable issues is spraying harmful chemicals on innocent plants and trees. Insecticides have evolved dramatically over the years, and are commonly used to prevent the insect infestation of plants. Although this process has pure intent, chemical spraying affects our environment greatly. Over 98 percent of pesticides reach a destination other than the targeted species. This contaminates all levels of the food chain, starting at the bottom with small insects. Every year before the Bing cherry trees blossom, orchard owners spray the trees to prevent aphids and other bugs from destroying the cherries. Most of the pesticides sprayed fall from the trees into runoff that can further damage surrounding vegetation and the soil's acidity. Acidity is crucial to the cherry trees. It allows for producing a bumper crop and overall, healthier trees. An abundance of crops means more capital for our economy!

Weather also causes Sweet Cherry tree destruction. During the springtime, the cherry trees are susceptible to frost, which creates a thin layer of crystallized dew on the tree. The freezing temperatures cut off the nutrient supply and affect the growth rate. Low temperatures can also result in cankers, which are sores that ooze sap. During growing season, strong winds are also a culprit of cherry tree demise. Winds can easily snap off healthy branches or uproot trees. An abundance of rain can produce over-grown cherries that will eventually split, becoming undesirable for consumption. The only safety method used today is the prediction of storms and their force. Many times storms cannot be weathered and preventive solutions cannot be found to avoid these situations.

A more recent concern is the aphid. Aphids are commonly known as plant lice, and have a variance of 4,000 species (about 150 species affect cherry trees). They are an eighth of an inch thick and usually wingless creatures; however, if the insect feels threatened, the mothers birth a generation of young that have wings. Their soft bodies can be green, yellow, red, pink or black. They also secrete a filthy, sticky fluid called "honeydew" that attracts molds. According to Teo Sprenger, a gardening specialist, the mold can take form as black knot fungus, brown rot, and leaf rot. The most common mold is black knot fungus, which can be treated by continuous use of fungicide. It is easily recognized by black galls that swell at the base of the tree's limbs. Aphids also cause damage such as leaf discoloration and stunted plant growth due to extracting sweet fluids from leaves. Aphids are hindered by their slow speed, allowing aphidophagous (bugs that feed on aphids) species to prey on them. Some examples of these species include lady beetles, lacewings, minute pirate bugs, hoverfly larvae, big-eyed bugs, damsel bugs, and certain stinging wasps. To overcome the damage of aphids, we can utilize harsh water spray, horticultural oils, and/or unleash their enemies upon them. We can blast them with a harsh water spray using the element of surprise against them. This method is not as effective as others, but is an easy way to reduce the population. We can also use horticultural oils to suffocate the bugs; however, the oils only come in small quantities. Lastly, we can release safe amounts of the aphidophagous species on trees to reduce the aphid population. However, meddling with natural population balance may backfire.

It is in our nature to nurture earth, and we must do what is necessary to keep her healthy. There are multiple effective and simple ways we can provide help for the Bing Cherry tree species. We can maintain woods surrounding the cherry trees by pruning dead branches and hauling the debris away. We can offer protection, such as fences and walls, to prevent storm damage and block animals from eating the sweet fruits. Avoiding fertilization during drought seasons will halt the response by putting out excessive growth when the trees should be going dormant. We can remove competing vegetation, which will also reduce fire hazards. Saving Bing Cherry trees will result in more growth for our already thriving community and create a chain reaction of awareness. It will also cause tourism to skyrocket, increasing financial capital. Our close-knit community has the power to prevail against hardships, and it is our duty as human beings and civil citizens to nurture the Earth. It is vital to protect the environment, and as it was once simply said by Naseem S., " If there are no trees, there are no humans."

The Door's Deer Damage
Written by Hanna Pierre

Although Door County's popular deer hunting season appears actively participated in, deer overpopulation remains an issue. Many residents and tourists travel to the county because of the vast woodland it provides—along with the plentiful deer population to hunt. Hunters love the immense quantity of deer, and many succeed in their hunt, yet the deer density continues to increase. With excess deer, many aspects of our beloved Door County have and will continue to deteriorate, resulting in a loss of agriculture and domestic plants, an increased risk of collisions with motorists, and a higher risk for disease.

Door County houses the perfect habitat for whitetail deer with its abundant woodlands and numerous croplands. Unfortunately, more deer inhabit the county than what is healthy for its carrying capacity. Dick Baudhuin, Door County Deer Advisory Council Chair, says "[Door County is] probably running somewhere in the area of 40 or more [deer] per square mile [of land], and for any kind of decent re-generation in the forest, you really should be down to 15 or less [deer per square mile]." This overabundance damages almost all of Door County, with Bauduin claiming "there [are] areas where [there] aren't as many [deer], and in some cases are few deer, but for the most part, all the way north to south in the county, we got too many deer." Both the DNR and local residents realize the abnormality of deer numbers where they live, but ignore the consequences.

With excess deer in the area, Door County's established agriculture will weaken. Deer scavenge for oodles of food each day, especially during the growing season when approximately six to ten pounds are eaten per day. With that amount of food required, many deer sneak into farm fields for peas, beans, and even strawberries—all crops produced in Door County. Many assume deer foraging in fields munch on grass, but they actually don't digest grass efficiently; they're almost always searching for planted crops. Locals, as well as national farmers, notice this issue, and have waived their right to take action. The Wisconsin DNR created a program called the Agricultural Damage Shooting Permit

Program which allows farmers to give hunters a limited number of tags to shoot deer that are damaging farmers' crop, both in and out of hunting season. Although this aids the limitation of agricultural damage, overabundance remains prominent. Not only do farmers suffer from deer damage, but resident's gardens and landscapes do as well. Backyard gardens provide a plethora of natural plants and foods; unfortunately, these attract deer and other hungry animals. Especially when a deer's natural habitat lacks an abundant food source, private gardens act as a magnet for deer.

An obvious problem recognized by almost all Door County citizens is the amount of deer related collisions in the fall and winter. The reason this time of year holds the record for the most motorist-deer collisions is because beginning in October, the "rut" season commences. Also known as the mammalian reproduction, deer during this time—especially bucks—are hyperactive and will dash onto highways without regard for vehicles. Due to the increasing density of whitetail deer in the county, the probability of hitting a deer, especially during autumn, increases greatly. The odds of hitting a deer in Wisconsin is 1 in 77 while the national average stands at 1 in 164. In 2015, more than half of Door County's reported car accidents involved deer. Perhaps the most eminent worry among local drivers proves the costs of

property damage. Many drivers carry auto-
insurance that will sometimes cover deer related
damage, but not always. There is an obvious cost,
whether it be replacing a headlight or fixing a dent,
but many do not realize the invisible cost of living
in a county with a large deer population. Wisconsin
is the seventh most deer-lethal state in the country,
and insurance agencies take advantage of it. They
calculate the probability that a driver will hit a deer
and use it as an excuse to raise rates. Not only are
vehicles damaged, but in some cases physical injury
may occur, if not death. The impact of a deer on a
moving vehicle may cause the driver to swerve,
increasing the risk of accidents with other drivers
and sideroad objects. In 2015, Door County, along
with four other counties, recorded a total of five
human deaths due to deer-motorist collisions. Each
year, Door County motorists are frequently warned
to be aware of deer near roads. Clearly, this deer
overpopulation causes the roads to be an unsafe
place for Door County drivers.

The abundance of deer increases residents'
risk for disease from the animals' many health
issues. Deer carry diseases such as CWD (Chronic
Wasting Disease), rabies, and anaplasmosis, with
the most frequent disease contracted being Lyme
disease. Over the last ten years, Door County has
reported over 50 cases of Lyme disease, most likely
derived from deer. Lyme disease in humans causes
a rash, along with flu-like symptoms. Left

untreated, it could become chronic, and in rare cases, result in death. The disease is spread by infected ticks, and many tend to reside on whitetail deer's coats. With the overpopulation of deer increasing, the hunters and residents of Door County are more likely to come in close contact with infected ticks hidden in deer fur. In conjunction, hunting dogs may host infected parasites, introducing the tick to their owner. Door County residents are cautioned to protect themselves and their pets from infected ticks living on the many deer in the area.

The consequences of overpopulation will continue to destroy Door County and the DNR recognizes it. They realize that "most hunters seek those adult bucks with big antlers, and it's difficult to get people to take antlerless deer and the adult does, because those are the ones that are reproducing." As a result, for the first time, hunter's licenses come with an additional five antlerless deer permit. In an attempt to reduce the amount of female deer in the county, the DNR created this opportunity. With fewer females present, the DNR hopes the deer density will decrease. Jeff Pritzl, DNR District Wildlife Supervisor, states that "[In 2017,] for every buck that's been harvested, we'd like to see at least two antlerless deer harvested." Willing hunters take advantage of this opportunity and aid controlling this overpopulated species.

This obvious issue of overpopulation must be recognized. Door County's deer population remains an issue for the environment and human safety. Local hunters are urged to help by hunting antlerless deer as well as male bucks during the season. With the DNR's help, Door County residents may continue to enjoy their surroundings without the hindrance of multitudinal deer.

AIR

"Clean air and a healthy climate benefit all of us, but it will take a diverse coalition to step up to the threat posed by unchecked climate change."
—Keith Ellison
Deputy Chair of the Democratic National Committee

Alternative Energy

Solar Energy: The Choice for Door County
Written by Seth Hanson

Most people think of solar energy as a clean, environmentally friendly way of saving some money on their electricity bill, but what exactly would it take for solar energy to erase that bill entirely? Solar electricity has the potential to provide Door County a clean source of energy that can provide residents and businesses major savings in as little as 10 years. Not only will solar energy decrease our dependence on fossil fuels and improve environmental conditions, but the reduction and eventual eradication of energy costs would bring more businesses, tourists, and full time residents to the county. Additionally, while there are significant environmental benefits, such as clean air, land, and water or the renewable nature of sunlight, there are certainly many other reasons to use solar panels. Unfortunately, there is no perfect solution, and lack of understanding along with implementation are both obstacles we must overcome. This being said, neither are deal breakers, and once we find a solution, solar has almost limitless potential.

To begin, what exactly are solar panels? Solar panels use the properties of photons, the light particles produced by the sun, to create a flow of electrons. Each panel is made up of small units called photovoltaic cells. These cells are made of a special class of materials called semiconductors—the electrons that form a small electric field. This field allows photons striking the cells to knock electrons loose, thus generating a flow of electrons, or electricity. By wiring these cells together, large amounts of energy can be produced. So far, the best solar panels available are only about 20 percent efficient, meaning that if the panel is hit by 100 watts of sunlight, it will only produce around 20 watts of electricity. Due to the constant advances in the field and increasing uncertainty about the future of fossil fuels, we can expect the efficiency of solar energy to rise considerably in the near future.

When it comes to powering an entire region with solar, there are two possible routes to take. The first is to install discrete systems on individual houses, taking advantage of the unused rooftop space. The second option is to build a solar farm, which would then generate power to be distributed across the existing power grid, just like with the current plants. Both options have positives and negatives which must be considered.

The first option—individual systems installed on a per house basis—offers many benefits. First of all, the space required would be minimal, since most of the panels would be installed on the roofs of houses and buildings that are for the most part unused. It would also be much more efficient than any available method of distribution, since electricity generated wouldn't have to be transmitted across power lines, where much of the power is lost.

On the flip side, despite their technical advantages, these systems do pose many logistical problems, especially in a place like Door County, with many rural areas and varied weather. The first potential problem would be paying for the systems. Unlike a centralized system, which could be paid for by continuing to charge for electricity at reduced rates, an individualized system would not supply the government any revenue to recoup the installation and maintenance costs. This leaves two ways to pay for the plan. The first is having individual households and businesses purchase and maintain their own systems. While this would, in theory, solve the cost issue, it would likely be more complicated than that. For one thing, many people may not be able to afford to purchase a solar system capable of powering their house, even with some sort of incentive like tax breaks or subsidies. Another problem would be that many people may simply refuse to purchase a system, upset at the idea of the government forcing them to buy something. Finally, maintenance would be an issue. It would have to be determined what, if any, responsibility the government has to maintain personally owned solar panels. Further, once that was determined, it could be problematic for anyone, private owner or government, to complete necessary maintenance on a regular basis. Here in Door County, one of the biggest issues would be snow, which would have to be removed after every snowfall. While many households could find it annoying or impractical to clear off the snow themselves, it would be all but impossible for the county to arrange for a system to remove all the snow, especially in rural areas. Also, while it is possible to set up systems that can keep the panels clear of snow and debris, they would drastically increase the cost of the overall setup. All of this assumes that the house in question is in the sun. In addition to this, each house would require a set of batteries to store power for when the sun is not shining. Many houses may be covered by trees or be in shade for some other reason. Although there are many environmental and efficiency benefits to this method, there are also many logistical issues that may prevent this from being the best option for a place like Door County.

That leaves the other option, one or more "solar farms," that collect solar arrays that produce, store and distribute energy similar to a conventional power plant. Of course there are several drawbacks to this method. As mentioned above, energy is lost as it is transported through a power grid. This means that more panels would be needed to make up for the lost energy, thus creating a larger impact on the environment, since it would require a large area of land to be set aside solely for solar panels.

While this method has fewer technical benefits, there are many practical upsides. For one thing, as previously mentioned, this method would make it easier to pay for the plants. Revenue would be made by billing people for the energy as it is distributed, and eventually phasing out the bills as the cost is covered to bring savings back to the consumers. In addition to this, since all the panels are in the same place, maintenance could easily be covered by a staff working at the plant.

One example of solar plants being used in Door County is a small solar plant built for Waseda Farms. They recently set up an array of 145 solar panels measuring three by six feet, expected to produce an average of 72,000 kilowatt hours a year, or about half the sites total energy consumption. If every business could do this, the result would be considerable savings once they paid off the initial cost of the panels. They were also able to make better use of their land, setting up the panels in grazing fields, which remain largely unused.

Solar energy has many drawbacks, just like any other form of energy. However, solar is one of the most promising options for a clean future. Since all the energy on earth can be traced back to the sun, it only makes sense to streamline that process as much as possible and get our energy right from the source. Also, while the initial costs may be high, we will soon see that it is worth it. Not only can solar cut down on our electric bills, there are also many economic benefits. A Door County powered by solar energy, without smog and pollutants, is a cleaner Door County, a smarter Door County, a more beautiful Door County. That's a place people will want to live and work. As the age of oil and coal comes to an end, solar power is the best bet for Door County's future.

Saving Sunshine

Written by Emily Koelpien

The most nourishing element of nature
The source of everything else
We wrap it up in metal
Like a present to ourselves

Sunny days or cloudy ones
Sunshine prevails
Even during power outages
Solar energy doesn't bail

We have panels on top of houses
And businesses, too
We really could have more
It's not difficult to do

Panels aren't big eyesores
They can blend in well—
Invisible to the eye
Or exist as artistic cells

Panels don't need their own
Dedicated space
They could be sliced in anywhere
With little wait

Solar energy powers more
Than buildings, of course
Solar panels can power laptops,
Cars, and more

We can buy panels,
Lease panels,
Install them for free
We can use energy,
Store energy,
Sell it back with glee

Solar energy doesn't cost more
Than coal or gas
So why not use
Panel power packs?

The Power of Wind

Written by Lexy Wery

Wind. People in Door County appreciate it for various reasons. It propels the towering sailboats through the beautiful waters; it alters temperatures to feel ten degrees cooler; it carries the sweet aromas of Door County throughout the area. However, it's rare to come across anyone who appreciates wind for powering their home. Because Door County's economy relies on a rich agriculture industry and tourists are drawn in by the natural beauty of the peninsula, we need to take steps to preserve our environment. Clean energy generated by windmills is a great course of action. It has always been a possibility in the county with near optimal conditions, but people have rejected the idea and haven't acknowledged the financial and environmental benefits. It is time we consider wind energy so it becomes a reality in Door County, rather than just a possibility.

Wind turbines carry with them considerable benefits that help to preserve our environment. Since the Kewaunee nuclear power plant's closing, Door County derives power from the fossil fueled Pulliam Power Plant in Green Bay. A lot of the pollution coming out of that power plant greatly affects the air quality here in Door County. Of course any prolonged exposure to pollution has devastating effects on people and the environment—both inland organisms as well as the aquatic life. Wind energy could reduce a portion of these unwelcome air emissions.

Though the problem of air pollution will continue to exist with the Pulliam Plant still operating, Door County could potentially spark a movement for other surrounding areas to follow suit with the construction of renewable wind energy. The way society is progressing towards the use of more earth-friendly energy sources, eventually the Pulliam Plant will have no other option but to shut its harming smoke stacks for good. Because Door County heavily relies on the wellbeing of the natural environment, any reduction of damaging pollution is a victory.

Not only are wind turbines environmentally friendly, but they are also financially beneficial.

According to the American Wind Energy Association (AWEA), wind has an annual economic benefit of about 20 billion dollars on the U.S. economy. Taking this into consideration, there is no saying how much Door County alone could economically profit from job creation, state and local tax revenues, and lease payments to landowners. Besides that, utility costs for residents would be minimized. The Office of Energy Efficiency & Renewable Energy states wind is one of the lowest-priced energy sources available today, costing between two and six cents per kilowatt-hour. Initially, monthly charges may slightly increase to cover the costs of construction, but long term utility costs would be cut in half. Even so, Door County residents should be able to justify paying a few more dollars a month short term in exchange for the long term preservation of the natural environment and the beauty it brings to the area.

Equally important, Door County has apt conditions to sustain windmills both physically and geographically. According to the Office of Energy Efficiency & Renewable Energy, large scale wind turbines start operating at minimum wind speeds of 8 mph and cut out at wind speeds of 55 mph. The county's annual average wind speed of 20 mph easily falls within that operating range. On top of that, Door County has a large rural community that could largely benefit from construction of a wind farm. In fact, new data released by AWEA shows that U.S. wind farms now pay 222 million dollars a year to farming families and other rural landowners. Because the construction of windmills is most successful on farmland, farmers could be financially supported by leasing their land while still being able to utilize it for growing crops or livestock grazing. With substantial incentives for the people giving up their land, finding locations to build would be easy.

Now that we understand the benefits of windmills, we must ask why there are no windmills in Door County. Currently, Door County residents have preconceived ideas that windmills are awful giants needing to be fought off. They think that wildlife such as the bird and bat population would suffer great losses from the spinning turbines. People are also concerned their property values will decrease because they think the sight of wind turbines is an eye sore and they generate incredibly loud noise. However, people don't have to go far to realize that their notions are false. Door County's neighbor to the south, Kewaunee, took progressive actions in 1999 with the establishment of Wisconsin's first wind farm. Though Kewaunee residents expressed dissent, a change of heart among the disputers occurred after the construction of the wind turbines. Andrew Nowak, a retired dairy farmer in the area, originally voted against the wind farms when he served on the zoning board. After they were put in place, he commented that he could live with them and the noise from the several turbines within a quarter mile of his home on a neighbor's property didn't bother him. Not only that, but four years later, a study by the Renewable Energy Policy Project (REPP) found "no significant evidence that the presence of the wind farms had a negative effect on residential property values" in the communities closest to the Kewaunee County turbines. As for the wildlife concerns, DNR conservation biologist and Office of Energy Shari Koslowsky stated the agency never received reports of any dead or injured animals near the turbines. This evidence refutes any antithetical opinions, so people need to have an open mind to the ways Door County could benefit from wind energy. Wind turbines are not harmful giants, but rather marvels of science that offer great advantages.

Door County is a special place. No matter the season, the natural beauty of the area is unable to be replicated. The scenery of the shorelines and surrounding greenery attracts tourists time and time again. Some fall in love with the county so much that they relocate to call this place home. Many farmers, on the other hand, call Door County home because they seek to sustain the rich agriculture established through years of hard work by previous generations. Nonetheless, the common theme among Door County residents is nature. Everything that ties people to this county connects

to nature in some way, thus finding ways to
preserve it is essential for future generations to
experience the area's beauty the same way we do
today. With Door County's greater good in mind, we
must conquer our giants one battle at a time,
starting with a switch from fossil fuel energy to
wind energy.

Temperature Change

Winter, Spring, Summer, and Fall?

Written by Deseree Dufek

It's winter in Door County...

But where is the snow?
The sun's blazing hot rays have melted away
The minimal snowfall bestowed upon us
In the past,
Snowflakes would fall lazily upon the ground and lie
there,

Starting in November and continuing throughout
February and sometimes into March
But as with other areas of life,
Door County changes
Our usually bitter-cold winter has disappeared
Replaced by unusually warm temperatures
And our consistent snowfall is nowhere to be
found...

It's spring in Door County...
But why has it come so early?
It's only February.
Yet our snow has left us barren,
And our cherry trees have begun to blossom their
delicate white petals
There is still a chance of frost, though—
A significant threat to our cherry industry
In the past,
Spring wouldn't arrive until almost April
The cherry trees wouldn't blossom until May
But as with other areas of life,
Door County changes
The spring we once knew does not align with our
temperatures anymore
Our warm temperatures appear earlier now
And our cherry trees are thrown into chaos

It's summer in Door County...
But why is Lake Michigan's water line so high?
Barely any beach exists along the shoreline

133

And the available space is overcrowded
It has rained more than normal this summer—
More than any other summer, for that matter
Feeding fungi that threaten Door County's apples,
cherries, and grapes
In the past,
Door County's beaches were wide, vast swathes of
sand
And rain was more scarce, too
But as with other areas of life,
Door County changes
This summer inundated us with rain showers we
cannot contend with
The unusually high temperatures
Have started to wreak havoc on our ecosystem

It's fall in Door County...
But why aren't the leaves changing color?
It's the beginning of October
And almost none of the leaves have started
changing color
The temperatures this fall have been unusually high
Suspending the trees' color change
In the past,
The leaves peaked at the end of September into
early October
And the temperatures were lower
But as with other areas of life,
Door County changes
This fall left us with a bland landscape

The leaves changed color at extremely unusual
times
Hinting at the larger issue at hand

Goodbye, Door County

Written by Hanna Pierre

Tourists from all over the world visit Door County to be enveloped in classy beauty that cannot be found elsewhere. The stunning hues of trees in autumn, iconic cherry crop, and waterfront beaches all contribute to Door County's attractive atmosphere. The untouched feeling of this area is currently losing its environmental allure due to air warming. Air warming continuously demolishes the vast beauty that Door County presents; we soon may say "goodbye" to the area loved by many.

Door County's picturesque autumn beauty is fading just as fast as the colorful leaves. Within the past five to ten years, especially in 2017, Door County has experienced unusually warm weather, banishing the excellence of the charming tree colors. Low temperatures spark the change in leaf color, and since it has been hotter than ever before, leaves have transformed later than normal. In order for the chlorophyll to react, the air must cool to between 40 to 50 degrees. Triggered by decreasing temperatures, chlorophyll ceases production, breaks down, and its green pigment fades. Shining through are xanthophylls and carotenoids—the vivid yellow and orange coloration. This year, the air did not reach the minimum temperature as soon as it used to. Early October's average temperature in 1997 was 48 degrees, while in 2017, the average temperature was a reported 57 degrees. The obvious air warming forces the leaves to transition later in the year, when the weather cools down. Warming continues to become more of an aggressive problem year after year, so eventually, Door County's colorful and ravishing autumn will push later in the year, and become non-existent.

Door County's exemplary cherry crop also suffers from the warm air epidemic. This area is famous for its thriving cherry production, attracting people from across Wisconsin and beyond into the peninsula. Unfortunately, with unusually warm weather and excessive rain in February, the usually perfect habitat for cherry trees is now ruined. Superintendent of Peninsular Agricultural Research

Center, Matt Stasiak, claimed cherry orchards lost fifty to seventy-five percent of their cherry crop in 2017—a misfortune for tourists, citizens, and farmers. In February this year, temperatures hit 58 degrees, allowing cherry blossoms to start and then freeze when winter conditions return, killing the crop for the spring season. Additionally, heavy rainfall contributes to the industry's failure. The average rain Door County received in June 1997 was 1.78 inches. However, in 2017, the area weathered a staggering 8.25 inches. With so much rain, it's almost impossible to control pests, especially for the succulent cherry trees. Farmers struggle with fungi assaulting the crop, and they claim disease pressure was twice as heavy. Again, air warming becomes more intense each year, so the Door County cherries that everyone adores will cease to exist in the near future.

The beach fun provided by the extensive waterfronts of Door County is also in jeopardy. Record breaking rainfall also threatens area beaches. After enduring extreme over-precipitation in June 2017, beaches all over the county were threatened by shrinking sand area more than ever before. According to Thomas O'Bryan (area engineer for the US Army Corps of Engineers' Lake Michigan Office), from 2013 to 2016, over four feet of water rose on the Lake Michigan Shores in Door County. He also claims this issue is the fault of over-precipitation in the area. Each year, the amount of sandy lakesides become increasingly scarcer. "The high water levels discourage people because they can't walk the beach," explains Tony Jeanquart from Town and Country Realty in Kewaunee, "Where there are stairs down to the beach, right now their first step is often right into the water." Clearly, these continuously worsening conditions are already affecting residents and visitors alike. In conjunction with growing rainfall, tourists and residents may be forced to say goodbye to that important aspect of Door County recreation.

It is obvious that due to air warming, Door County's many iconic qualities will cease to exist in the near future. The captivating area tourists and residents know and love is endangered; having been damaged by humans, it is only humans who can restore it. Saying "goodbye" to our area's most admirable traits surely is not ideal, yet we allow air warming to demolish our beloved county.

Unseen Pollutants

Vehicular Air Pollution: A Major Mist-demeanor

Written by Megan Neubauer

Each year, tourists travel from all over the Midwest to visit the beautiful and natural Door County. According to the Door County Visitor Bureau, in 2014 alone, Door County's tourism industry contributed to an astounding 313.4 million dollars, something many locals take advantage of. While at first this number is to be celebrated, the ongoing issue of the vehicular air pollution that

these very tourists produce should raise concerns.
The amount of pollution from tourists' vehicles
contributes steadily to Door County's ever-growing
smog problem. At first glance, one may argue that
the real problem with the vehicular air pollution
stems from the use of off-road vehicles like dump
trucks and tractors; however, the constant overuse
of cars and trucks during Door County's hottest
months constitutes most of the peninsula's air
pollution.

The amount of pollution each vehicle
contributes to the air largely depends on the type of
fuel and model of vehicle. Fuel types include regular
gasoline, diesel, and other alternative fuels.
According to the Wisconsin Department of Natural
Resources, on average, Wisconsin's highway traffic
emits thirty-three million tons of carbon dioxide
per year, and off-road vehicles contribute an
additional three million to that sum. However,
clean gas options do exist. Regular gasoline can be
reformulated into a cleaner gas. Only thirty percent
of the United States uses reformulated gas. This
number could easily be increased in Door County. A
small change to the type of gas used has the
potential to institute a large change in the future.
Diesel fuel, on the other hand, is already a highly
regulated industry. In fact, most off-road
productions must use an average sulfur content of
15 parts per million, a number safe for the
environment.

141

With so many regulations and alternatives, what's the big deal? Chemicals called hazardous air pollutants (HAP), the very chemicals emitted from our vehicles, include carbon monoxide, volatile organic compounds, methane, hydrofluorocarbons, and nitrogen oxides. These chemicals cause a higher risk of cancer and damage the immune, neurological, reproductive, and respiratory systems, affecting almost every part of the body. Ninety percent of the carbon monoxide in the atmosphere comes from modes of transportation. Smog, a thick layer of air pollution that resides in the lower level of the atmosphere, consists primarily of volatile organic compounds and nitrogen oxides. Forty percent of volatile organic compounds and sixty percent of nitrogen oxides stem from the use of cars and trucks. The worry for air pollution in Door County centers around smog, filled with detrimental effects for humans and similar to regular air pollutants. However, because smog lies in the part of the atmosphere where we live, the chance of experiencing its effects increases drastically. Smog causes premature death, aggravated asthma, immune system depression, and cardiopulmonary problems.

Recently, the Environmental Protection Agency (EPA) presented their rising concern for Door County's smog levels with a push to add another smog level monitor in addition to the one already located in Newport State Park. This machine records the ozone level of the area chosen by the EPA and sends the information to the Department of Natural Resources. The EPA uses the received information to monitor the amount of toxic air parts per billion in Door County. The EPA requires specified territories to remain below a certain number of parts per billion. In 1979, this number was a staggering one hundred twenty parts per billion, but since then, the number has dropped to allow only seventy parts per billion (EPA Air-Quality Concerns Reach Door County). The drop in parts per billion has Door County on a "nonattainment" status, forcing our county to follow a strict set of rules, including smog fines and highly regulated factories.

It's obvious Door County experiences smog, but how is it possible that such a tiny and sparsely populated area could be so concerning? Tourism perpetuates the problem. With a massive number of tourists traveling during peak summer temperatures, vehicle emissions melt into the ground and evaporate straight into the ever-growing smog cloud, where it can be deadliest. This is just the beginning, though. Another growing problem lies in the proximity of Chicago in relation to Door County. Winds filled with vehicular pollutants from Chicago follow Lake Michigan and sit not far from the shores of Door County. These winds, trapped between the cold lake water and the warm atmosphere above, can only travel to the side, soon mixing with the air over Door County. This leaves Door County with more air pollution problems than Chicago itself.

In 2015, Door County faced five smog violations, marking nine total days of breaking the federal smog standard. After this violation, Door County experienced a crackdown on rules and payed a hefty fine. In the future, businesses might relocate to where air pollution laws are much less restrictive, causing a substantial drop in the local economy. Since Door County residents pay for these violations, it's imperative we recognize the problem at hand as a major issue.

Door County Visitor Bureau's Spokesman Jon Jarosh says: "People expect air quality alerts in a place like Chicago. It's frustrating to see in an area like ours that has no ability to control what's happening, but maybe that reminds people why we all need to be good neighbors." So as a good neighbor, what can be done? To start, citizens must take a stand against power plants and factories refusing to burn cleaner, natural gases. The problem begins locally. Door County citizens need to stop the growing smog level. Individually, we can use fuels that burn cleaner, especially the correct kind of diesel gases which include 15 units of sulfur or less. Being a smart shopper helps, too. When looking for a new vehicle, consider the many benefits of purchasing a car that includes a new brand of tailpipes, one that helps a vehicle emit less smog-related chemicals.

Overall, if the change starts with Door County natives and moves to everyone who loves our precious county, the results could be incredible. By informing those around us of the ever growing issue our county is facing, we must take action together to attain the needed changes. If we used some of the money our tourists bring in, we would be able to make substantial improvements to the environment. As we rely on tourists for income, we also recognize they are part of the problem. It's a vicious cycle for Door County, one we need to break.

Black and White

Written by Emily Koelpien

The first canvas is thought to be
That of cuneiform
The first story
Recorded
In clay

Those forget
Of the canvas
Which shows itself every night
And disappears each day

The sun, the stars, and the moon
Are three celestial bodies
That connect every person
Who has ever graced the Earth

The stars have told stories
The stars have connected people
When language did not

The stars have guided travelers
The stars have connected people
When maps did not

The stars are our original guide
But
Our guide has left us

Not of his own free will
We've forced him out
We've blinded him
Our bright lights
Have cast him into
A black abyss

Yang is too big
Yin is no longer balanced

The impact is growing
Our daytime pollinators cannot pick up
The slack their nighttime friends
Can no longer accomplish

The Earth is feeling the heat
From excess pollution
And the sickening amount of light

That stains the planet each day and night

Excess light
Disrupts natural flow
Doesn't prevent crime
Costs a lot of money
And for what?

How I Wonder Where You Are

Written by Zoey Kohler

"Twinkle, twinkle little star, how I wonder what you are." We grew up wondering what the glittering lights across our night skies could possibly be; however, light pollution threatens to extinguish the Milky Way from our view as well as alter circadian rhythms, disrupt wildlife, and signify energy waste. Without care, nothing will be left of our dazzling night skies but legends.

Light pollution is defined as excessive, misdirected, or obtrusive artificial (usually outdoor) light, and affects more than just star visibility. Excessive artificial light interferes with melatonin production and therefore the body's natural circadian rhythm, throwing off sleep cycles and leaving us feeling restless. Commonly known as the sleep-regulatory hormone, melatonin also suppresses tumors, meaning light pollution could raise cancer rates. Already a 2008 study at the University of Haifa in Israel found increased instances of breast cancer in women who live in light-saturated neighborhoods.

We are not the only ones who rely on light moderation. Critters, especially those that are nocturnal, depend on light and dark during their daily life and seasonal cycles. For example, migrating birds navigate using the stars at night during spring and fall migrations. Bright city lights can be confused for constellations, resulting in entire flocks lured by the urban glow. Each year, as many as 10,000 birds crash into windows, resulting in death or injury leaving them vulnerable to predators.

In addition to migratory birds, sea turtle hatchlings confuse the bright lights of civilization for the moonlit glow of the ocean. Misdirected towards land rather than the safety of the water, these tiny turtles end up eaten by predators or dying of exposure.

Other animals wait for the cover of darkness in order to feed and breed. For species such as snakes, frogs, and salamanders, lunar cycles dictate activity levels. In times of darkness, these animals fill up on prey and call out for mates; however, they prefer to find shelter when the landscape is illuminated to stay safe. Artificial lighting increases periods of hiding, meaning animals eat and search for mates less frequently. Populations of nocturnal animals are decreasing due to starvation and lowered reproduction rates, and research shows that it doesn't take stadium lights to cause an impact. Even distant or soft lighting alters creatures' routines.

Bright lights from metropolitan areas diffuse a great distance, resulting in what is known as "sky glow." This glow, created when light reflects off of moisture and dust floating in the air, hovers over cities as a dome of squandered illumination. An estimated 80 percent of the world's population and 99 percent of the United States population lives under skyglow, an extreme case of light pollution. Luckily, unlike some environmental issues, light pollution is easily and quickly reversed.

Simple actions, when implemented by the masses, accumulate to significant reduction in light wasted to the heavens. By placing coverings over outdoor light sources and directing bulbs downward, we already see a positive impact in our night time skies. A less desirable, but still effective, solution is to reduce use of decorative lighting during holidays and celebrations. Often these lights are left on for countless hours, which pollutes the skies with light as well as fritters away energy.

151

Another option is to simply turn off lights when not in use. This is the cheapest, easiest, and most effective method of dealing with the problem. If safety is a concern, then automatic timers or motion sensors can be installed to use light appropriately.

Colored lighting exists as a lesser known option. Yellow, red, and amber lights reduce glare and effects on night time vision. Because the lighting is less harsh, colored bulbs are kinder on the eyes and have lesser effects on circadian rhythms, all the while keeping our stars bigger and brighter.

Approximately thirty percent of generated light in the United States ends up wasted to the skies. Pointed skyward, it washes out the stars while dangering people and creatures in the glare. Thankfully, simple adjustments to light fixtures and usage will save star-glittered skies, animal lives, and energy costs.

The International Dark Sky Association designates lands "possessing an exceptional or distinguished quality of starry nights and a nocturnal environment" around the world. Recently Newport State Park on the tip of the Door Peninsula was added to the list of 48 dazzlingly dark skies, the first in Wisconsin and the third in the Midwest. We must continue light preservation tactics in order to maintain this honor in our park.

Ultimately, protecting our starry skies comes down to preserving a piece of our humanity. For generations, the galaxies acted as a navigational tool, and constellations helped pass on stories of the past. As stated by David Crawford of the International Dark-Sky Association, "We human beings lose something of ourselves when we can no longer look up and see our place in the universe." We must protect our night skies full of bright, beautiful stars or else future generations will be left wondering where they are.

WATER

"For many of us, clean water is so plentiful and readily available that we rarely, if ever, pause to consider what life would be like without it."
— Marcus Samuelsson
Head Chef of Red Rooster in Harlem, New York

Chemical Contaminants

Hydrargyrum

Written by Deseree Dufek

Defined by its protons—80 in total—mercury
Isolated at room temperature, a liquid silver
blob—quicksilver, to some

Toxic vapors flow off this substance,
This brilliantly deceiving substance, dazzling us
with its rich color
So beautiful
Yet deadly

When someone breathes in mercury vapors,
Acrodynia may ensue
Affecting the nervous, digestive, and immune
systems
Systems key to our existence,
Without them, we die

It is a naturally occurring substance, you say
We cannot avoid it
It will always appear in our everyday lives

It is a result of human activity, too, I say
We can minimize the amount in our environment
By reducing the products containing mercury

At one time, we used mercury in our everyday lives,
like in thermometers
But we have realized our err
Or have we?
How come this toxic element resides in our waters?

Lake Michigan, central to our lifestyles, contains
this pollutant in high enough levels
It has been placed on the impaired waters list
Along with Mackaysee Lake on Chambers Island

Coal-fired power plants, like those in Green Bay,
release inorganic mercury into the atmosphere
Eventually falling into the waters we love the most

If we don't put a stop to this problem soon we all
will be mad as a hatter

Pesticide Use in Lawn Care

Written by Alexis Jandrin

Most Americans readily picture the same ideal lawn. People imagine vibrant green grass with flowers of every color strategically placed throughout the yard, complementing each other perfectly. There will usually be trees scattered throughout the yard, providing shade for those who want to play underneath. What many people don't realize while visualizing this paradise is the work put into achieving the modern American "perfect lawn." Most Americans spray pesticides over entire lawns in an attempt to eliminate weeds that pollute

161

their vision. In Door County and all over America, many people fail to acknowledge the plethora of side effects associated with the use of pesticides. The Door Property Owners, Inc. has recently informed Door County residents about some negative consequences of pesticide use on the environment and living organisms. Ultimately, ensuring a safe and healthy lawn is up to us, the homeowners.

In reality, most people are aware there are many negative effects of pesticide use. The most commonly known result of pesticide use is seepage of the chemicals into the ground when sprayed. These toxic chemicals eventually get into well water, contaminating whoever drinks from it. No matter how scary that may be, many people don't consider the other side effects of pesticides. Once spread onto our lawns, the chemicals are capable of contaminating other waterways such as creeks, lakes, and rivers. As a result, a multitude of problems occur for wildlife. For example, when male tadpoles ingest pesticide-related chemicals, they undergo a sex change. It's clearly a red flag if a chemical can physically allow a male frog to mate and produce effective offspring. On top of sex-changing frogs, other types of terrestrial life malform due to the exposure of pesticides. Countless types of birds, fish, and microaquatic organisms, that are essential members of entire food chains, cannot survive the accidental consumption of pesticides. That being said, the popular new class of insecticides amongst major pesticide companies, neonicotinoids, now immobilize and slowly kill its consumers. Neonicotinoids target the nervous systems of insects leading to paralysis and eventually death. The Environmental Protection Agency (EPA) suspects neonicotinoids to be responsible for the rapid decline of pollinators, especially the honey bee. Pesticides do not only directly affect the insects that consume them, but also indirectly contaminate the animals that depend on insects for food. In 2006, the bottoms of caves were found covered with dead bats. Scientists believe these bats died due to weakened immune systems, and discovered neonicotinoids to be the culprits.

Recently, studies have shown the use of pesticides increases the risk of cancer in children. Scientific data proves that children contaminated with pesticides are forty-seven percent more likely to develop leukemia, and forty-three percent more likely to develop lymphoma. Another study stated girls introduced to the chemicals in pesticides before puberty were five times more likely to develop breast cancer, and exposure to pesticides for children in the womb quadruples their chances. Young children exposed to pesticides have increased chances of developing numerous, and potentially fatal, cancers. Hazardous chemicals in pesticides cause cancer in a multitude of ways, such as damaging DNA, altering genes, disrupting hormones, and provoking tissues.

The President's Cancer Panel claims, "Exposure to these chemicals is widespread." Pesticides have become the norm, people no longer stop to think about the consequences of the chemicals within the environment and themselves, but rather how well of a job they do killing unwanted organisms. Cancer survivor and biologist Sandra Steingraber relates cancer to pesticides in the President's Cancer Panel report by saying "[People] have sprayed pesticides ... throughout [the] environment. They are now in amniotic fluid. They're in [people's] blood. They're in [people's] urine. They're in [people's] exhaled breath. They are in mothers' milk ... What is the burden of cancer that [people] can attribute to this use of poisons in [the] agricultural system? ... We won't really know the answer until we do the other experiment — which is to take the poisons out of [the] food chain, embrace a different kind of agriculture, and see what happens." Humanity must acknowledge pesticide use as problem rather than a necessity for an aesthetic looking lawn.

What many people are unaware of how easy it is to avoid the use of pesticides and still maintain the "perfect lawn." In Montgomery County, Maryland, there have been attempts to ban pesticide use for lawn care; however, the state of Maryland overruled this new policy. Many

Montgomery County residents claimed banning pesticide use in one county will eventually lead to the ban of pesticides throughout the state. Even so, many "perfect lawn" owners did not have faith in the proposed bandwagon effect that would be generated by just one county implementing this law.

What many people in the state of Maryland failed to realize was how simple it is to live a pesticide-free life. Many countries in the U.S., including Door County, have looked at Montgomery County as an example and aspire to follow the pesticide ban. The Door Property Owners, Inc has made it a goal to educate property owners on how to make safe decisions about properly maintaining their lawn. The most important step in maintaining a perfect pesticide-free lawn is monitoring one's property very carefully. Other important steps include testing soil, reseeding regularly, fertilizing or adding compost, and watering frequently. For some people, these simple steps may still sound like a lot of work compared to spraying pesticides. For those people, maintaining a chemical free lawn while still routinely spraying every spring can soon continue, due to a recipe change in Ortho's products, a major pesticide company. In the year 2021, the companies will not contain any harmful chemicals, such as neonicotinoids, in any of their products. This allows people to keep the ease of using pesticides and maintain the perfect lawn, without all the unwanted chemicals.

All in all, pesticides are extremely dangerous. Not only do they harm the environment by polluting water sources, killing pollinators, endangering frogs, and weakening other animals, but they also significantly increase people's risk of cancers such as leukemia, lymphoma, and breast cancer. Pesticides achieve all of this destruction in organisms by manipulating their nervous systems, DNA, genes, hormones, and tissues. Why do we insist upon using these fatal chemicals to obtain the "perfect lawn" when it is so attainable to create the perfect lawn without them? Perhaps for the lack of knowledge or the ease of chemicals? Either way, people must stop using pesticides in Door County, America, and the world to preserve not only the environment, but also the human race.

Lead
Written by Deseree Dufek

Seeping into our water through the pipes we use to
pump it
We ingest this toxic substance
Not realizing its effects on our bodies
Affecting our brains in irreversible ways, this heavy
metal ruins our lives

Five micrograms per deciliter of blood harms a
child
Or so the EPA claims

But is any amount of lead worth the loss of our
thoughts?

Beware, Citizens of Door County!
Is lead in your water?
Seeping into your bloodstream?

Wreaking its havoc on your system?
Destroying your mental capabilities?
Eating away at your brain?

Why must it come to this?
What is the issue?
Where does this evil come from?

Products made with lead, like lead pipes, are the
greatest culprits
So switch your lead pipes out for copper, PVC, or
any other kind
Rid yourself of that flaking, harmful metal

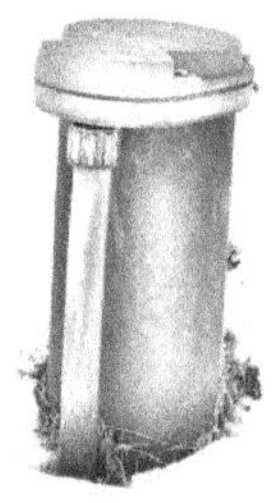

Reeking Havoc in Our H_2O

Written by Kalin Glesner

Upon the arrival of any living thing; water is most essential to keep us alive. It is important to realize where our water comes from and what we put into our system because at birth 80 percent of our body is water, and by adulthood it is still a significant 70 percent. As Door County samaritans, it is critical that we remain aware of the detrimental effects our behavior has on the water that has lasting effects on our survival.

Although most people living in cities have a public water system, nearly 850,000 of private well owners in Door County do not realize that the sanitation of their well depends on how well they tend to the system. Up to 70 percent of residents rely on groundwater as their main drinking source—a source that is polluted by pesticides, feces, and other harmful products. Most are unaware of what they are putting into their systems, and oblivious to the fact that it isn't healthy.

An extensive collection of data gathered by the county revealed that of 682 samples taken, a stunning 254 didn't meet regulations. Those that didn't meet standards contained between 2 and 20 mg/L (milligrams per liter or parts per million) of nitrate-nitrogen. These findings indicate that the use of land has affected the quality of our groundwater. In addition to the 254 impaired samples, 19 more were deemed unhealthy drinking water as the result of excessive nitrate-nitrogen levels. Exorbitant amounts of nitrate emanate from manure spreading, fertilizers, and legume cropping, and the discovery of immoderate levels of the compound in our water point to a serious problem for our county.

Detected in numerous Door County wells, arsenic has also become an issue threatening the safety of residents. Of 72 water samples collected, 100 percent of them contained an alarming amount of arsenic. The drinking water limit of detectable arsenic was lowered to 10 µg/L (micrograms per liter or parts per billion). Is it justified that standards are lowered just to make ends meet?

Based on research done by the Wisconsin Water Science center, Door County's water received a score of just 20 on a 100 point scale measuring water quality. Although this is not data on the water that comes from your faucet, it is data on the water from Door County's watershed (an area or ridge of land that separates waters flowing to different rivers, basins, or seas).

If the chemicals in our water isn't alarming enough, in 2014, seven Door County visitors required hospitalized due to the water they were bathing in. The manure from a large farm nearby had spread into the water of the private well. Most would like to believe that the point of bathing yourself is to get clean; however, in these unfortunate cases, the manure in the water was so grim that it resulted in violent illnesses. Although the violent illnesses weren't specified in these specific cases, a common illness due to the sewage is campylobacteriosis (bloody diarrhea, cramping, vomiting).

Door County has long been deemed a beautiful vacation spot for both summer and fall, and our income thrives on the tourism that our aesthetic home entrusts with us. Nevertheless, the water quality and the effects it has had on our visitors could drastically decrease the amount of travelers we see in our area. Without a doubt, our economy and citizens would struggle due to decreased revenue generated by the tourism industry.

It is our duty, for the sake of future generations and future visitors, to keep our waters free of harmful bacteria. It is a topic that can no longer be ignored. It must be discussed and investigated, but most importantly, it needs to be combatted before it becomes irreversible.

We are Made of Chemicals

Written by Deseree Dufek

At least 55 percent of our bodies
Consist of water.
Without H_2O, we could not survive.
Wait, H_2O?
Isn't that...
A chemical?

What does this mean?

We are full of chemicals.
Oxygen, carbon dioxide,
And water.

Our every cell contains chemicals.
Not every kind is good.
Not every kind is bad.
It begs the question:
Where do we draw the line?

We are made of chemicals—
Which are good?
Which are bad?

Are pesticides "good" chemicals because
They help us mass-produce crops?
Or are they "bad" because
They contain toxins
Which shouldn't enter our bodies?

Some toxins are so prevalent,
We cannot escape them.

We are full of chemicals.
Oxygen, carbon dioxide,
And water.

We are full of chemicals.
Lead, arsenic,
And mercury.

Some chemicals throw our bodies
Off-balance.

Some help stabilize our bodies.

We are better off without
Poisonous chemicals.
Yet companies still produce,
Market, and distribute them.

How much longer must we suffer
Before we learn our lesson?

We are full of chemicals.
Oxygen, carbon dioxide,
And water.

We are made of chemicals.
Hopefully the kind that help us,
Not hurt us.
Water Pollution

Sunken Treasure

Written by Emily Koelpien

Normally one has to find treasure
Rarely does it come to you
Typically, treasure that comes to you
Is a gift
But this was no gift

This "black sand"
Hot "sand"
Expelled from a black boat
The remnants of coal
Used to propel forward

While the people on board have a good time,
The animals down below,
The people swimming about,
They most certainly are not having a good time
No, they're being poisoned

For decades upon decades
Warning upon warning
The SS Badger continued it's tyranny
In 1952
We created our own doom

In Sturgeon Bay, it was forged
In Lake Michigan, it lives
It's twin, the SS Spartan
No longer swims

Composed of heavy elemental metals
The debris is carcinogenic and neurotoxic
This "black sand," so the SS claims,
Isn't bad at all
So for decades, the coal ash was fed to the fishes

Their coal ash contains lead, barium, arsenic,
mercury
But not a lot
Not enough to hurt anyone
Or anything
So they claimed

The EPA finally stepped in
Gave them the ultimatum
Stop pollution or stop running
So they added some pipes
And recycled the ash into cement.

Good.
Genuine good change happened.

"Life isn't for going fast.
Life is for enjoying the ride.
And this has been delightful,"
Mary Lou Deutsh said

Hopefully the poisoned ash
Hasn't drained the force out of too many lives
And hopefully the ride
Was worth its consequences
Hopefully the ship's catering and the Wi-Fi
Makes up for the poisoned water supplies
Hopefully the ash
Never harms anyone or anything again
Hopefully.

Microplastics in Lake Michigan

Written by Ben Kielar

Half of the plastic dumped into the Great Lakes goes into Lake Michigan (11 million pounds), which is approximately 100 Olympic-sized pools full of plastic bottles every year. Just one plastic bag can quickly break up into 10,000 tiny fragments. In general, people overlook the effects of human progress on the environment as the man made world moves forward. More specifically, the effect on Lake Michigan is forgotten, allowing microplastics and microfibers to quietly wreak havoc on its flora and fauna.

Microfibers produced by consumer goods negatively affect the environment by their presence in lake water. These debris particles are microscopic strands of synthetic fibers from clothes that incorporate polyester, nylon, and acrylic, as

179

well as fishing nets, bottle caps, and plastic bags. One fleece jacket can produce 1,900 new fibers each time it's washed; multiply this by 75 jackets being washed throughout the county and the result is a staggering 142,500 fibers! These microfibers are then pumped into rivers and lakes with treated wastewater, since they aren't entirely strained out during the water cleaning process. Being numerous and invisible to the human eye, they are hard to detect and manage. The only way to control them is by preventing them from ever getting into the lake, but this is easier said than done, since most microfibers are microscopic. One would think that microfibers already in the lake could be extracted in order to protect aquatic life, but only an ultrafine net would collect enough fibers to protect these animals. Further, such a net would also ensnare the microorganisms on which many aquatic species thrive. Microfibers are also difficult to eliminate because of the wide variety of consumer goods they are found in.

As microbeads build up in Lake Michigan, they become a greater hazard to the health of aquatic life and, in turn, human life. The Great Lakes are awash in tiny spheres of polyethylene and polypropylene (both types of plastics), which companies have been adding to toothpaste, hand soap, and exfoliating facial scrubs since the 1990s. Lake Michigan alone contains 17,000 microbeads per square kilometer, and that number is constantly growing. These microbeads, like microfibers, are unable to be completely separated during wastewater treatment, and are, consequently, pumped into rivers and lakes unencumbered. Although polychlorinated biphenyls, or PCBs (industrial products or chemicals), were banned in 1979, they still affect us today because they remain in the environment for a long time.

Since microfibers are not biodegradable, they can linger in the water for hundreds or even thousands of years. Furthermore, these lingering microfibers and microbeads have the propensity to absorb toxic materials, posing a serious threat to both humans and wildlife. With no way to extract them, they biomagnify year after year. These tiny pieces of plastic trash have large surface areas for their size, which allows chemicals and bacteria to build up. In some cases, chemicals absorbed by microplastics concentrate at a higher level than the water around them. Therefore, when a fish inadvertently eats them, they lodge in the stomach and intestines, and there is an increased chance that the toxic hitchhikers will cause harm. If edible fish contain deadly chemicals, the humans who consume them will undoubtedly ingest them as well. In one study, researchers indicated that while microbeads can potentially pass through a fish's digestive system, microfibers become enmeshed in a fish's gastrointestinal tract. This study also revealed the presence of microfibers inside a double-crested cormorant, a fish-eating bird common in Door County. Once inside an animal, the chemicals and toxins which the microfibers absorbed while in the water can eventually become absorbed by the animal. From microorganisms to humans, the effects of microplastics can make their way up the food chain. The pollutants on microplastics often concentrate in the organisms that ingest them, like plankton and fish. When these are consumed by birds or humans, the microplastics contaminate their new host, posing health threats from the chemicals, bacterium, and viruses accumulated on them.

Microbeads affect aquatic plant and animal life alike, for when they enter lakes and settle to the bottom, they choke the plants, disrupting entire ecosystems that aquatic animals depend on for food and cover. Additionally, aquatic animals mistake microbeads for fish eggs and eat them. This causes plastics to build up in their stomachs, which eventually leads to starvation because they aren't ingesting the nutrients they need to survive. Aquatic animals are at risk to lose not only their habitat, but their ability to reproduce. According to researchers, Peter Eklöv and Oona Lönnstedt, some young fish prefer plastics over their natural foods, and have started ignoring the smell of predators, causing them to starve to death or be eaten before they reach reproductive age. Recently, scientists have also observed stunted growth and increased mortality rates in fish exposed to plastics during their development. Chemicals attached to microplastics find their way into fish and other lake animals and seep into the bloodstream, leading to the potential of crossing the blood-brain barrier, causing neurological damage. These effects can be detrimental to food chains, habitats, and the checks and balances that control the populations of the entire Lake Michigan ecosystem. Man Made interference can destroy nature's delicate equilibrium, and that will be the consequence if the issue of microplastics is left unattended.

The issue of plastics polluting Lake Michigan is largely unknown by the citizens of Door County, affecting them in ways they are unaware of. There is great need to educate Door County residents and residents in all of the Great Lakes watershed. This pollution produces detrimental effects that could become irreversible; which is why we must challenge companies who produce products that contain microfibers and microbeads to use natural alternatives, like ground fruit pits; a natural biodegradable alternative that does the same job as synthetic microbeads. There are millions of pounds of Door County and Michigan tart cherry pits available as a local and natural substitute. Any of us can be a part of this movement by supporting microbead free companies, advocating for natural alternatives in products that use microbeads, making our own organic products, buying fewer

clothes that contain synthetic fibers, and reducing
usage of one-use plastics, such as plastic bags,
straws, and styrofoam containers. Once people are
informed about this crisis, change will occur. The
condition of the environment is dependent upon
the behavior of the humans that inhabit it. If we
don't take action, we can't complain about the
consequences of a problem that has been neglected
for decades.

Plague of Impassivity

Written by Emma Jeanquart

Home is where the heart is. Parents embody that heart. Mom and Dad: wherever they are, that's where you belong. Home personifies our parents.

Laid out before you stretches a shore, garbage lining it like lace, spreading out in a web. Some places thick with trash, others sparse and empty. A smell permeates the air, releasing wafts of pungent, rotting flesh. Amongst the refuse manifest the decomposing, rancid bodies of every type of fish

185

you've ever seen. Even the scavengers feeding on the decay appear just as diseased. The water appears cloudy, murky, completely fouled. Can you see it? Feel it? The horror of this water embodies our future.

Not to offend, and I promise I knocked on wood while writing this, but imagine if your parent became sick in the worst way, with cancer. Bare with me here. Let's think about what causes cancer. It's our cells. We contain only cells. When a couple of them become corrupt, they start attacking each other. Our body attacks itself.

Living in Door County, our home exists by water: our 'body' of water. As inhabitants of this body of water, we may consider ourselves cells. To be honest, we're really crappy cells. We pollute with no thought. Chemicals alter the ecosystems and destroy the safety of a limited freshwater source. We assult our home.

We represent cancer. We destroy each other and our surroundings. Our will to change our behavior ceases to exist at the moment, for only few can see the ruination.

We decide, if only through indifference, to not dispose of things properly. Voluntarily, we decide to ignore what slight regulations exist to protect the environment. We forget *our* ownership as well. We allow our home, our mother, our father, exposure to poison.

Door County is a tourist destination, sought after for its beauty. Diminishing beauty, that is. Sickness grips our home with patience and cunning, eating away from the inside. A stranger walking past you would be unable to detect sickness, but someone who interacted with you regularly, would. Door County's situation is identical. Aware of the disease, locals detect changes to a greater degree; they affect us the most. According to data collected from the year 1918 to 1998, the water levels experience an increase with each long term water fluctuation. With shores full of zebra mussels and nothing else, we notice. In the years 1993, 2005, and 2008, zebra mussles have been found in Door County waters such as Little Sturgeon Bay, Sturgeon Bay and its canal, Kangaroo Lake, Clark Lake, and Rowleys Bay. The threat this invasive species poses to the ecosystems surrounding the peninsula could be explained by a civilian off the street, because one of the most prominent industries in Door County is fishing. Our home suffers, alongside the fishing economy, and soon the tourist economy as well.

Why have we let these issues go unaddressed? We care, don't we? If so, action must be taken. We need to save our home from the consequences of our neglect. Pretending is no longer a viable option, and soon sickness will overtake our home in the most obvious and detrimental way. Our waters, the backbone and body of Door County, will be toxic. Home is where the heart is; our heart has been poisoned by neglect. To save it, we must not ignore the problem any longer, by recycling, conserving, and protecting the waters of Door County.

Agriculture and Aquatics

A Future Filled with Phosphates

Written by Deseree Dufek

A green algal bloom spreads across the water's
surface,
A strange sight so early in the summer
The toxic waters dissuade me from swimming,
Not to mention,

The water's vile stench repels me from fifty feet
away,
Despite the wind's unwavering silence

The carcasses of dead and bloated fish bob on the
water's surface—
Casualties of the water's dead zone, an area where
oxygen is sucked out of the water by bacteria
decomposing the dead algae
It's a vicious, continuous cycle of living and dying
The greater the algal bloom, the larger the dead
zone,
The more dead fish in the water, the greater the
stench in a once beautiful place

As this scene unfolds before me, I ponder the effect
on future generations
When comes the day that no more fish live here,
No more fishermen fish here,
No more children swim here,
No more frogs hop here,
No more...
Except the pukey-green algal bloom covering the
once-blue water

191

Living With CAFOs: It's a Crap Chute
Written by Gracie Englebert

Before indoor plumbing became standard in the 1930's, people in rural American communities like Door County utilized chamber pots or outhouses; however, today most of us don't give a second thought to its convenience. Even fewer of us stop to consider how the system actually works—where does the waste go after we flush? In small towns, most homes use a septic system. Septic systems utilize a two-tank technique in which the solid waste is held in the first tank and the liquids pass through to the second. In the first tank, bacteria break down the solid waste, but the liquids from the second tank are simply discharged into the ground. The ground should work as a natural filter, catching the solutes so the liquid reaching the groundwater is pure. However, for this process to work, it's important for the soil to be a mixture of sand, clay, and gravel. If the soil only contains one or two of these components, the liquids won't be properly filtered, which results in contaminated groundwater. To prevent this issue, the Clean Water Act requires homeowners to pass a soil inspection before installing a septic system. Additionally, there is a field size requirement determined by the number of bedrooms in the home—the purpose being an area of soil large enough to efficiently filter all of the liquids emitted by the household. Finally, mandatory leakage checks are issued every three years (failure to do so results in a large fine) to ensure the system is in proper working order.

Although it appears that we are being protected from contaminated water, most farms remain exempt from the Clean Water Act. They aren't required to undergo the same soil tests or leakage checks that homeowners are. Although this wasn't a large issue in the past, Door County (as well as its neighboring counties) is beginning to suffer the effects, and the leading contributor? "Progressive" agriculture. According to the United States Census of Agriculture (USDA), the number of dairy farms in Wisconsin fell from 62,836 farms in 1982 to 29,908 in 2012. However in the same timeframe, the number of cows per farm increased from an average of about 71 to 117. The shift toward fewer farms with more animals results in more condensed operations, or CAFOs (concentrated animal feeding operations.) While there is only one registered CAFO in Door County, the fifteen Kewaunee County CAFOs affect the lives of thousands of Door County residents. Years ago, when more small farms were spread over a greater geographical area, the soil was able to handle the amount of manure being spread. Additionally, farmers use to spread manure in its solid form, so decomposers could break it down over time while it remained on the surface of the soil. Now, modern farmers prefer to save time by spraying manure in its liquid form, but liquid manure seeps into the soil more rapidly than solid manure. As a result, the waste cannot decompose quickly enough to avoid reaching the groundwater. To further compound the issue, far too much manure is being sprayed onto fields, and the soil, supersaturated, cannot filter it fast enough. The result: liquid waste contaminates our groundwater as well as our surface waters.

Water supports all life on Earth, but Door County's relationship with water is even more intimate. Surrounded by Lake Michigan on three sides, our peninsula depends on water to keep the economy afloat. From fishing to shipping to tourism, water is absolutely essential to Door County's thriving economy, which is why it's paramount to keep it clean. Unfortunately, tolerating irresponsible farming practices allows

CAFOs to poison Door County's lakes and rivers. However, containing only one within our own borders, we must look south, toward our neighbors, to find the source of the pollution. In 2016, the Ahnapee River was the only Door County river, lake, stream, bay, or brook to be placed on the DNR's List of Impaired Waters. In contrast, all three of the rivers traversing Kewaunee County (Kewaunee River, East Twin River, Ahnapee River) earned a spot on the list. Surely it's not a coincidence that the only Door County river shared between the two counties earned a spot on the list. In each case, the contaminant responsible for the impairment was phosphorus—a highly water soluble inorganic compound abundant in cow manure and easily transported as run-off. While decomposing fish bones and granite rock sediment are also sources of phosphorus, neither inflate phosphorus thresholds to the point of contamination. But what's the problem with high phosphorus levels anyway? After all, as a nutrient, phosphorus aids plant growth in the soil as well as in the water. However, bodies of water containing too much of this compound experience rapid algae growth that often covers the entire surface. Not only does this block sunlight from penetrating the surface, it also sucks all of the oxygen out of the water when algae naturally begins to decompose. It may seem strange that algae, producing eighty percent of Earth's oxygen, is extracting it from the water; however, algae intakes oxygen from the water when decomposing and outputs oxygen into the air as a byproduct of photosynthesis. With decreased levels of oxygen in the water, fish essentially suffocate, leaving behind what scientist call a "dead zone." Further, algae-covered lakes and rivers are a blemish on the beauty of Door County that attracts tourists from around the country. In 2015, the tourism industry fed 18.2 million dollars into our county's economy. Without the great fishing and aesthetic pleasures Door County currently offers, the economy will suffer.

In addition to tourism, agriculture has proven vital to Door County's economy for generations. From famous Door County cherries to small family farms and CAFOs, we rely on agriculture to provide more than just food: orchards and farms provide jobs to thousands of residents. But how do CAFOs change the role farming plays in a rural county like our own? Most people know that CAFOs produce more efficiently than small-scale operations, which is what allows us to buy food at far lower costs than smaller competitors can offer. Unfortunately, this benefit is quickly turned into a disadvantage when the numerous family farms that used to thrive disappear, only to be replaced by a few oversized enterprizes. Furthermore, CAFOs typically don't buy or sell at the local level. They import feed and equipment from large corporations and, similarly, market goods to non-local establishments. In short, CAFOs do not stimulate local economies and may even cripple it after they subjugate most locally-based operations.

Even more alarming than the threat CAFOs pose to our wildlife and economy, though, is the threat they pose to the lives of Door County citizens. In surface waters alone, residents and visitors may be exposed to any number of pathogens (a specific causative agent, such as a bacterium or virus, of disease) carried by animal waste. While overabundant levels of phosphorus in the body can cause kidney damage, this mineral is perhaps the least alarming. Salmonella and Escherichia Coli (E. coli), both transmitted into water by cow manure, have far more startling effects. Salmonella, to which children are more susceptible than adults, may result in fever, chills, diarrhea, or abdominal pain. E. coli may cause bloody diarrhea, intestinal infection, dehydration, kidney failure, or even death. In fact, an average of one out of every twenty E. coli cases will end in fatality. Door County citizens and their children are at risk of exposure not only when swimming in the beautiful water that surrounds Door County, but also any time they consume fish or shellfish caught in local waters.

While it certainly isn't fair that some locals—fearing for the safety of their family—are forced to avoid some aspects of life in Door County, what is worse is that some citizens are not safe in their own homes. In fact, the USDA states that

197

contaminated drinking water exposes consumers to over 130 waterborne pathogens. To further the issue, these pathogens actually survive better in groundwater, as it is the perfect environment (dark and cool) for them to thrive. And people neighboring CAFOs are not the only ones at risk of contamination. Wells in Door County are typically just short of 200 feet deep, but some reach up to 600 feet below ground. With wells this deep, the water coming out of your faucet could be coming from streams miles away, streams contaminated by waste from CAFOs. In order to protect against the contamination of drinking water, households must first be aware that they are at risk. This is not the case for many Door County residents who are oblivious to the fact that a CAFO twenty miles away may be polluting their water. However, even if residents are privy to this issue, the Center for Disease Control (CDC) recommends "regular testing of household water wells" to stay on top of the problem. The other option citizens may choose is to install a reverse osmosis filtration system to ensure the purity of their drinking water. Both methods, though, prove extremely costly, and therefore highly impractical for a rural community. Water tests may cost up to 150 dollars per test and reverse osmosis systems cost twelve to eighteen thousand dollars per home. Although many people claim nothing is free, it seems ridiculous that we must pay to be safe in our own homes.

Perhaps the only insurmountable struggle citizens living near CAFOs face is the absolute annihilation of their property's value. Even if they avoid the wonderful waters of Door County and ensure the safety of their drinking water by paying thousands of dollars, they cannot escape the traffic, noise, and odors that come with CAFOs. While most people would ask why they don't simply relocate, the unfortunate truth is that they can't. According to the CDC, property value can decrease up to 88 percent within one tenth of a mile from a CAFO. In other words, a home once worth 100,000 dollars can plunge to a value of only 12,000 dollars. There is simply no way the vast majority of homeowners could afford to relocate after experiencing such an extreme deficit. Essentially, they're trapped living underneath the oppressive, smelly foot of a huge farm. However, it is not only those living near CAFOs who are being affected. Every citizen living in Door County is suffering because we are tolerating the problems caused by the willful ignorance of factory farmers more concerned with increasing their own profit than the safety and well-being of our community and environment.

Idle

Written by Deseree Dufek

Rain falls
Upon the liquid manure coated fields.
Once idle, stinking manure
Now flowing through the fields
Following the river
Towards Lake Michigan.

A brown swirling current
Laps at the shoreline
Filled with contaminants.
This mess does not belong here
Along the sparkling, pristine coast.

Nature never needed
Unnatural manure

To blossom and grow.
Nature cares for itself—
Evident in every season,
Every life cycle,
Every ecosystem.

Dead plants and animals
Contribute to the soil
Which young plants use—
Growing strong and wild and free.
Plants provide sustenance for nature's
Wondrous creatures,
Who eventually return to the soil.

So who is responsible
For that brown swirling current?
Why do we suffer
From dirty drinking water
And poisoned soil?

We have no choice;
It is forced upon us.

Is that really true?

What else can we do?
We live in a country
Where placidity isn't common.
The minority normally brings attention to itself.
But where is the minority in our community?

No one speaks about
Our water's contamination.
We notice,
But do nothing.
"Why do we have this problem?"
We wonder,
Sitting along the riverside,
Idle.

A Miracle

Written by Anna LeBrun

We take for granted
We control
We disregard the wrongs
For what?

To suffer in the next life
If there is a next life
To force the next generations into suffering

We control
We disregard

The choices we make for this earth
Things we shouldn't have touched
For what?

To exterminate
To terminate
The rights of living things
The right to live
For what?

To make our lives more comfortable for a while
Only then to have caused a small, unnoticed war
A war of chemicals on plants
To rid the trees of bugs,
To rid the skies of birds,
To rid the water of fish

For what?

Life is a miracle, hard to comprehend
A one-time chance to get things right
We take for granted
We control
We determine
Which pests live and die

Life is a miracle
Slowly being exterminated by life itself
In the hands of humankind

The Threat of Man-Made Drought
Written by Anna Meier

"Rain is grace; rain is the sky descending to the earth; without rain, there would be no life." John Updike aptly described the importance of rain and precipitation, for without precipitation, an area of land becomes parched and barren, and the disastrous consequence: withered crops. Droughts in Northeast Wisconsin have never reached an extreme level, but they still threaten the area. While a man-made drought has not yet struck Door

205

County, Northeast Wisconsin has three potential causes: irrigation systems, deforestation, and greenhouse gases. As citizens of Door County, we need to continue our efforts to be proactive in eliminating the threat of man-made droughts.

Droughts, by definition, occur because less than expected precipitation falls on an area, and/or the precipitation is not correctly introduced into an ecosystem. However, careless and excessive irrigation, deforestation, and greenhouse gases also cause man-made droughts. Dr. Anne Van Loon of the University of Birmingham summarizes the importance of researching man-made droughts in order to prevent them: "Managing drought effectively means we must acknowledge that human influence is as integral to drought as natural climate variability. This is why we're calling for research to explicitly consider the multi-directional relationship between natural drought processes and the role of people."

Droughts in Door County could have severe economic, agricultural, and social impacts. Most notably, during the Dust Bowl of the 1930's the precipitation for Door County was 28.53 inches below the average of 31.05 inches. According to Dick Kalnicky of the Wisconsin DNR, this led to crop failure, economic decline, and health problems due to lack of food and proper nutrients. Today a severe drought in Door County would negatively impact the agricultural-based tourism industry.

Locally-sourced restaurants would have trouble acquiring necessary supplies. The blossoms of fruit trees would wither, leading to little or no fruit crops. The dairy and cheese industries would literally dry up as lack of adequate forage would lower the milk production of cows. All of these industries and businesses would face drastic economic losses and potentially shut down, causing the deterioration of vital tourism revenue for Door County.

Excessive irrigation causes droughts because the demand for irrigation water exceeds the amount of water available. For example, California recently suffered a compounded natural and man-made drought when the "Salad Bowl of America" overextended its water resources, permanently damaging its trees and soil.In Door County, the current irrigation systems are for vegetable crops, potato crops, and landscaping and tree businesses. One landscaping and tree farm has a long history with irrigation. According to David Meier, a lifelong resident of Door County, a severe drought struck in 1976, and the plant production center improvised its irrigation sources. It drilled a well cased to 300 feet, the same depth as the City of Sturgeon Bay's wells, but took too much water out of the municipal reservoir and had to file paperwork to get permission to draw water from Lake Michigan when rain finally came. This leads to another issue—the Lake Michigan water level. A drought would lower the level of the beautiful lake that residents of Wisconsin depend on for tourism, fishing, drinking water, shipping, and shipbuilding. A drop in the lake level would result in fish death, lower clearance for ships, issues with piers and marinas, and fewer tourists to produce revenue for Door County. If these factors go unchecked, they can result in a man-made drought.

In addition to the potential problems caused by irrigation, deforestation can also lead to man-made droughts. People cut down trees for a variety of reasons: to clear farmland, to make firewood, to hunt, or for better land management. In the 1850's, the trees removed by original settlers of Door County were used to build houses and settlements. Later, in the 1870's, commercial logging in Door County cleared large areas of land. However, the settlers and lumber companies did not realize that this act endangered their land. The act of removing trees adds to the carbon dioxide in the air, causing global warming. According to Jim Robbins of the New York Times, cleared land also provides more surface area for water to evaporate and lessens the potential water retention of an ecosystem. This leads to decreased capability for the precipitation of an area to positively impact the ecosystem and eventually causes a man-made drought.

Just as deforestation leads to man-made global climate change, the global warming itself leads to man-made droughts. Greenhouse gases trapped in the atmosphere cause a 'blanket effect' on Earth—trapping heat and causing global warming. Widespread global climate change leads to man-made drought by eiverting jet streams (high altitude bands of strong wind that jets fly in) that carry vital precipitation to areas of land. The local jet stream loops air from Western Canada into the American Midwest, bringing with it cold and wet fronts. Global climate change easily affects jet streams, for the warming of the climate creates more distinct and varied waves of the jet streams, resulting in more extreme weather patterns. In and around Door County, the largest greenhouse gas emitters are the Green Bay paper mills, Green Bay power plants, large farms, and, of course, gas powered vehicles. In Door County, cars and motorized vehicles are the fastest mode of transportation up the long and narrow peninsula. Environmentally, these factors contribute to the greenhouse effect causing global climate change and, inadvertently, man-made droughts.

Economically and socially, agriculture is vital to Northeast Wisconsin. Since the aforementioned factors are man-made, and therefore preventable, everyone in Door County can and should do something to prevent or counteract them. In order to counteract deforestation, Door County-based groups such as the Door County Land Trust and Crossroads at Big Creek, have formed to protect land through nature preserves. Also, the CRP

(Conservation Reserve Program), a government created program, has offered monetary incentives to farmers who plant trees on former agricultural land. These groups are successfully protecting and replanting trees in Door County. While there is no legislation on the use of water for agriculture in Wisconsin, an example of such legislation is the Iranian water rights. To prevent drought from over-irrigation, Iran has laws in its constitution that necessitate a permit and fee for any agricultural use of water. Similar laws could be used in the United States to control and monitor irrigation systems. Another way to prevent man-made droughts is to reduce carbon emissions from personal use and power plants. A recent study found that legislation that sets goals and caps for carbon emissions effectively reduces those carbon emissions. Individually, people can reduce their carbon footprint by insulating their homes, recycling paper, driving less, and eating locally sourced foods.

As citizens of Door County, we must continue to support these groups and legislation and proactively manage the threat of man-made droughts. We must continue to preserve Door County, whether economically, socially, or agriculturally, because man-made droughts endanger all aspects of Northeast Wisconsin.

Save Our Sister

Written by Emily Koelpien

Today is officially the worst day of my life.

Worse than heartbreak, worse than family problems, worse than everything. And no, I'm *not* being melodramatic.

Okay, maybe I am a little. We're moving today. Moving to *Door County*.

Ugh.

So my family used to live there, right? About a decade ago, we moved for many reasons. For one, my parents weren't huge fans of the tourists. It became impossible to go anywhere during the summer due to overcrowding. Restaurants always had a wait list that exceeded an hour, boutiques were packed elbow-to-elbow, people recklessly crossed streets. Often, we were required to travel for hours to a location to enjoy ourselves. A lot of the beaches in Southern Door, where we lived, became overgrown, tiny, and just weren't any fun. The further north we drove, the better the beaches became, but then we were further away from other things that we wished to enjoy. For example, you'll find a beautiful, expansive beach, and thankfully there's an ice cream shop close, but then there isn't a pizza place nearby without driving across the peninsula.

First world problems, I know. "Oh no! If you find a halfway decent park to bring your kids to, you're too far away from any of the stores that you want to go shopping at! If you go to a town that has a lot of great restaurants, then you're far away from a movie theater! The horror!" I just didn't like how spread-out things became, you know? Certain towns became known for certain things, so other towns just stopped trying. Travel time between towns became excessive, meaning the need for a car became exponentially necessary. It's baffling how there wasn't any public transportation that ran connecting town to town. Door County became known for each tiny town having a specialty. Sturgeon Bay became known for its chain stores and chain fast-food. Egg Harbor became known for its unique restaurants. Ephraim became known for its unique boutiques. Sister Bay became known for its music scene. You get the idea.

213

All-in-all, though, I didn't mind. I liked the driving. It takes a while to drive from one sector of a bio-city to another, why wouldn't something similar exist in Door County? Instead of concrete, however, nature connects the separated towns.

My parents did mind, however. The roads and the towns became too congested. Too many people clogged the streets and sidewalks when it was nice, and the frigid atmosphere and terrible roads resulted in too miserable a condition when it was bad. So when my mother fell sick and my dad lost his job, we left Door County within days. This was a decade ago.

So why go back?

Well, we don't really have any other option.

*　*　*

On my lap sits an envelope. Unopened. I couldn't open it. "Happy 18th Birthday, Jason!" is written across the front. It's from my mother.

My father, sister, and I were all piled into the car, barreling seventy miles down the highway. My sister was preoccupied with her book, and I with the window. Our father drove. We left our previous apartment early this morning and have been driving for nearly eight hours, but we were almost there. I've been watching for signs along the road indicating our progress, and I've noted that we should arrive to Door County in about forty minutes.

So close.

We were moving into our uncle's old home. The house sat in the outskirts of Southern Door, and it's free. He moved to a house in the suburbs of a bio-city. There is a humongous waitlist to move to a bio-city because, well, everyone wants too. They're the peak of health. My uncle's previous house (the one we're moving too) has been in the family for generations. I recall it being in good condition, back when we'd gather there for holidays and whatnot. I also recall when my dad told us we were moving back to Door County.

"Really?" He was on the phone with my Uncle Richard. Dad's face was painted with disbelief. "You're giving it to us?"

"What are we getting?" Kristen (my sister) asked. She's still in elementary school. I'm very protective of her— she's a tiny little ball of happiness with tightly wound hair and the biggest smile. She also has the biggest appetite and the tiniest attention span. "What's for dinner?"

Dad waved her off. "Sounds good, Rich, I'll take you up on your offer. This place is too expensive for me," his head scanned the room, pondering. There was a pause, some vague grunts, and then he ended the call.

I was sitting at the dinner table. "What was that about?"

"Well, actually, due to some... circumstances, we'll actually be moving into my brother's old house because he's moving west. Arizona, I think..."

"Oh, why is he moving to Arizona?" I inquired.

He paused in his advancement towards the fridge. "I'm not really sure. Guess I didn't bother asking." Then Dad opened the mostly-empty fridge and took out a plastic bottle filled with water. "I was just too excited that he offered us the house. Our father would've been disappointed if it wasn't in the family anymore—" a pause, his face tight in concentration "—But now I'm wondering why he seems so... eager... to leave. He's moving out by the end of the month."

Kristen hadn't said much of anything. She held her stuffed bunny in one hand (dragging it's body along the floor), and a cup with apple juice in the other. She sat next to me, placing the two items in front of her. "What's going on?"

Now Dad sat down opposite Kristen and I. "We're going to be moving to Door County. We used to live there before you were born, Kristen," he glances to me, remembering. "It's a very beautiful place where most of our family used to live. Now a lot of them have left, so we get to live where they used to. Do you understand?"

"Yeah!" Kristen's face was painted in absolute delight. "Do I get a bigger room?"

"Well, of course!" Dad confirmed, glad she was on board.

I, myself, held conflicting feelings towards returning. I mean, we left for a reason. Economically, we were struggling, so I'm not sure why our situation now would be much different; and environmentally, I recall hearing things were starting to become questionable. Evidentially, that must've been a false claim, because Dad wouldn't voluntarily put our health at risk. So, I packed up my life, helped Kristen pack up her life, and after two weeks, we left our old lives behind.

*　*　*

Remember when I said that the environment going downhill must've been a false claim? Turns out I was wrong.

Very wrong.

In the mal-city that we used to live in, there were bouts of acid rain. You always wear a special jacket if you *must* be outside when it rains, a face-mask from time to time— nothing serious. Nothing more serious than any other mal-city in recent time, anyways. That meant there really weren't trees or flowers around, and buildings started deteriorating faster than how they used to, but overall, the city was beautiful in its own architectural way.

As we're driving though, I'm trying to recall my memories from when I was younger. I assume the fields outside of the Door County are empty because it is early spring and nothing has grown yet. I struggle to recall if the water in the bay was always as muddled and… green… as it is right now. I assume the trees just hadn't started growing leaves yet. I forgot that early spring was still supposed to feel mildly cold. Once we started to become more engulfed in nature, the more I realized that the once-vibrant natural landscape that made Door County a must-see is now rotting from the inside-out. The grass's hue is a sickly, dead, muted green. The sun struggles to shine through the permanently-foggy air. No birds take to the skies. For the remainder of the car ride, I watch nature die around me.

*　*　*

The LaSalle property has been in the family for generations. It was traditionally passed from parent to first-born, which unfortunately wasn't my father, yet here we are. Arriving at our new house, we bring all of our boxes in. Of course, we only unpack what we need when we need it, so many of the boxes sit untouched for weeks. Dad was hired at the bank, and I started working in a big store, so Kristen often spent her time with the neighbors.

I notice that nearly every week, at least one person calls in sick at work for multiple days, and typically isn't fully recovered when they do come in.

Half of my co-workers looked like zombies for weeks, with pale yellow-tinted skin, often wheezing after carrying literally anything, bruised up, and would explode into coughing fits. The coughing makes me cringe.

"What's going on with everyone? They look dead," I comment. I'm working with Tyler, who thankfully wasn't a part of the zombie horde.

"No one is entirely sure. Maybe something is going around," he absentmindedly continued working, as if the condition of half of the staff wasn't concerning.

"Have you gotten sick like that?" I asked him, opening boxes for him.

Ironically, we were stocking over-the-counter medicines. "No, I haven't. No one in my family has, thankfully. If it strikes one person, it usually gets to the whole family pretty quickly, so I hear. It's odd, because it doesn't appear contagious."

"I wonder what causes it," I stated out loud. I can tell Tyler surprisingly doesn't seem to care. He just wants to finish his shift and get home. Understandable.

I am still a bit horrified of my co-workers' condition at work, which I explain to my father as I prepared dinner. He didn't seem too interested either.

"People get sick, Jason, I don't know what to tell you!" He is exasperated with me. "People in our old town were sick all the time! It's a part of life!"

"I don't think people got sick like this before, though, Dad," I tried to explain. "Half of our team is out consistently!"

He didn't care, and wanders off to another part of the house to work on unpacking boxes and whatnot. Defeated, I returned my attention to my meal, prepared exclusively with bottled water, as well as boxed and canned foods. Nothing fresh. Nothing is ever really fresh. We'll use frozen food often, when we can.

The rest of dinner went by in a flash. Dad took his plate to wherever he was working, Kristen took hers to her room, so I retreated with my plate to my room as well. I sat down to eat at my desk, where my mother's envelope sat unopened—untouched, unread— on the desk. You see, she left everyone little presents (or instructions on bigger gifts) for years to come.

My letter would be the first of many handmade gifts and letters to open.

I feel like I can't do it. It's too much pressure. That letter could contain absolutely anything, and, by opening it, a part of her mystery dissipates. So it sits untouched, just barely out of my reach, on the opposite corner of my desk.

Soon, a tiny rapping on the door ensues. I take off my headphones and open the door to my sister's giddy face. "Want to go outside?" She inquires, putting on her brightest smile. I always made sure to get her outside when I could. So many of her peers sat inside, wasting their lives, as their mental and physical health deteriorates as they stare at screens, a dirty hand in a bag of junk food. Not Kristen. She's actually very healthy for someone her age.

"Yeah, Kristen! Let me grab The Bag."

"The Bag" is an emergency pack, and everyone carries them whenever they go outside for fun. Otherwise, a smaller pack is commonly carried.

We head outside.

The door closes behind me with a definite *thud.* Instantly, I'm blinded by a radiant sunset. The sun burns with a deep orange color. It tints the slight haze that lingers just above head a heavenly golden color, letting occasional streaks of light shine on the ground, similar to a natural spotlight. Once my eyes adjust, I see the malachite-colored waves as they crash violently against the shore. Kristen is already a good distance ahead of me, running like her life depends on it.

There is a big maple tree in the middle of the backyard, just before the shoreline, and the vivid memories of climbing it when we came up to visit return to me. The cousins and I would pretend we were escaping pirates and needed to scamper up the tree as fast as we could. Most of us made it to the top— I know I always did. There was no stopping me. I was the king of climbing trees!

I affectionately held a hand against the bark, remembering all of the times we ran around its base, playing tag or something similar. Now, even though it's the middle of spring, it is leafless. It has taken on a muted hue that trees don't typically acquire unless they're dead. I'm able to break off a branch with my bare hand using minimal effort. I guess this tree suffers the same fate as everything else has.

"Jason!" A tiny voice screams out from far away.

I look over from the dead tree branch in my hand to Kristen, who's on the beach. She's sitting on the beach, specifically in the path of the lapping water. Her left leg juts out and she's holding a hand over a large patch of it. Once I'm closer, I can see that she's managed to scrape it.

The dirty, polluted water is running over her open wound.

"No, Kristen!" I scream, dragging her back by the armpits, out of the touch of the water. Now she's crying. "What did you do?"

She is rubbing the gash with the palm of her hand. "I fell in the water by accident and I— I..." she sobs, she's grasping at breath, "I fell on a rock. It really hurt."

"I'll say," I place a hand on the square of her back, pulling her hands away from the wound. I pull

the emergency bag off and grab the supplies I need.
After applying some disinfectant and antibacterial
cream and a band-aid, we just laid under the sun,
soaking in the rays. Silence hung heavily between
us.

*　*　*

Kristen fell sick.

She was laid up in bed for weeks with a fever.
She wriggles on her bed, tossing and turning, her
face pinched. She's constantly sweating. Disposable
plastic water bottles lay littered around the bed, the
garbage overflows with tissues, and empty plates
with crumbs lay on dressers and chairs. I'll bring
her food for every meal that I'm home, but I've been
working overtime in order to help pay for doctor's
bills. So has Dad.

There are so many pollutants in the water. I
did some research on how Door County's
environmental health managed to deteriorate so
much, and I was shocked.

"I couldn't believe it! They stopped testing
the water. How could they just stop?" I was grilling
Tyler while we were stocking shelves.

"I guess it got so bad that it wasn't worth
trying to fix it?" He offered half-heartedly.

"Didn't you go swimming when you were
younger?" I asked him, remembering when I,
myself, went swimming in the water at my the

house. It was always a hot summer day, with a blazing bright sun and a cloudless sky. I would run around with my cousins. We would cry out about how hot the sand was under our bare toes. We would fall to our knees once we encountered the water and feel its cold fingertips graze our legs as it receded back into the bay. As fun as it was to be on the beach with my family, I always wanted to bring my friends up here. Especially for my birthday. The thing is, I would want my friends up here for a warm summer day, but my birthday is in spring. Nevertheless, when I ran on that beach, I imagined my friends were behind me and we were playing a game of tag. We would build a really awful sandcastle and than pretend to be giants and we would demolish it. We would swim and splash each other to the point of declaring a game of war and we would split up and try and swim as sneakily as we could and surprise the opposite team. Afterwards, soaking-wet, we would eat hotdogs and hamburgers with chips and dip and soda— the classic beach cookout.

Tyler snapped me out of my state. "Yeah, I guess, but it was kind-of polluted when I was younger. I mean, the water was green and I just didn't like swimming in it. So I've stuck to pools since then. Didn't you just move here?"

"Well yeah," I told him snappily, dropping my box back onto the cart, "but my family is from here. The water was never great, but it sure has gone downhill fast."

"It's probably because they started pushing water activities."

I looked to him. "Started pushing what?"

"You know," he started, opening up the box that I just dropped, "Like ferry rides up to Washington and Rock island. A few boats run all day long, all summer long, as opposed to only one that used to run. And now, there is a really big company right by the docks where you can rent motorboats and waterskis and things like that. There are a lot more people on the water now than there used to be. You know, people that own yachts and whatnot. Oh, and there was a ship that came into the area that needed repairs because it had an oil leak. That was huge. That was a year or two ago by now…" He was concentrating on trying to squeeze a box past the other rows, and it was a narrow fit.

"So because of all of the activity, the…" I struggled to think straight, "DNR? They stopped testing?" I moved onto stacking another row.

"I guess. I don't think they really tested much before, anyways. I remember my dad telling me that there was some new push for even more tourism here. More cars, more traffic. Great… right…? Ha!" He found the right angle to squeeze that box past the others. He moved onto the next row. "So yeah. They closed down the beaches, but still had water activities going. Oh, but they stopped fishing. I really miss salmon. My family always had fish-boils around the Fourth of July, and it was so much fun.”

”Dude, that does sound good,” I told him.

“It was,” a pause. Tyler stands up and looks at me face-to-face. “So how’s Kristen?”

“Still just as awful. Whatever is in her system from the water really doesn’t want to leave. But I think she’ll get better. The universe has already taken so much from me,” I had to look away from him as tears well in my eyes, “I know it can’t take Kristen away too— like it took Mom away. But she’s in pain— I know it.”

“Maybe your mom is lonely up there?” Tyler offers, putting an arm around my shoulder.

“That doesn’t help!” I push him off. “I don’t even *know* what I would do if I lost her too! She’s—” a shudder passes through me, making my shoulders and back convulse. The tears unfortunately slowly piddle down my face. “She’s the most important thing to me— and Dad, too. I don’t— I don’t even know what I would do without her.”

I ended up going home early from work. Tyler was very apologetic, but it wasn’t his fault. I brought Kristen a candybar and water bottle before retreating to my room. Sitting on my desk is the envelope I received on my birthday.

It is from my mom.

It is from before she passed. I didn't know she had left us all gifts, so when I saw her trying-too-hard-to-impress-you "fancy" handwriting, with the date in the corner and "Happy 18th Birthday, Jason!" across the front, I almost started crying then as well. The sting of her absence feels ever-present. It's been months, and I miss her just as much as I did when she left us.

Today is the day that I'm going to open her letter.

I carefully slice the top of the envelope open, attempting to preserve it as best as I could. I was surprised to discover that there wasn't a letter inside the envelope, but rather, a postcard of Door County. It was of a field of cherry trees. The petals were actually the classic baby-pink, borderline white, little buds that explode out of the tops of the trees. I inadvertently take in a sharp breath, shocked at the image. The trees are how they should be— healthy and full of life. The grass is freshly cut in rows, and is extremely green. The sky is a healthy, natural blue, with fluffy clouds that hang above the treetops. I flip the postcard over to see the note that she wrote me.

Happy Birthday Jason!
I probably won't be there to celebrate it with you, but I know you'll be alright. Eighteen is a big milestone! Now you're an adult. At least that's

what you'll need to tell yourself until you're about thirty and THEN you'll actually be an adult.

I know you'll look after Kristen. I was surprised how well you two always got along, but I'm glad you both love each other so much. I can just picture you two with families of your own, getting together for the holidays, and you'll be just as close then as you are now. Take care of your dad now, alright? I'm not sure how well he'll handle you leaving for university, but at least he'll still have your sister for a couple more years, before she's off too. Make sure you visit him, okay? He's very family-oriented. He'll miss you guys.

I'm getting ahead of myself. Today is your birthday, and it's your special day. I hope you have fun with your friends. Don't get into too much trouble! I know you're a good kid. Not to boast, but we raised you well.

I love you so much, Jason!

P.S. I have gifts planned for you for the rest of your life. You'll never have to worry about missing me. I'll always be right here in the pages of these letters.

P.P.S. I'm not sure if your dad told you, but you're going to be moving into Uncle Richard's old house up in Door County. It's really beautiful up there! We moved away because we really needed a more condensed city, but I know how much you loved walking the trails and going swimming at the beach. Make the most of it! I know you'll love it.

Maybe you'll even want to move back there once you're out of university. I know your dad would want you to.

P.P.P.S. I know I already said this, but Happy Birthday! I love you! Until the next gift...

There are blotches on my jeans from the tears that rolled down my cheeks. I put the postcard down onto the desk again, careful not to get too many fingerprints on it. I calmly walk to Kristen's room and stand in her doorway, watching her.

It's been weeks. She hasn't gotten much better.

I don't want to watch her suffer anymore.

I know what I have to do now. I have to change the laws around here. I have to start a movement to clean up the water. I have to do something.

Something. *Anything.*

Restoring Door County's beauty, like how it used to be in the picture, is possible. It has to be. But it's a community effort.

I sit down at her desk, pick up a pencil, and start to write:

Save Our Sister:
A proposal about cleaning up Door County's water...

Meet The Authors

Gracie Englebert
Editor-in-chief
Contributions: The Legend of the Orchid and Living with CAFOs: It's a Crap Chute

When I was younger, I thought all people were fortunate enough to experience four unique seasons. As I grew up, I began to understand and appreciate the miracle of frigid winters that melt into mild springs and sweltering summers that smolder into fiery autumns. Now, I refuse to part with the aspect of Door County that I love most. I refuse to remain passive as carbon emissions rob the trees of their trademark fall colors or as pesticide misuse annihilates the delicate cherry blossoms seen all around the county each spring. I refuse to watch environmental abuse destroy our seasons.

Deseree Dufek
Text Editor
Contributions: Winter, Spring, Summer, and Fall?,
Hydrargyrum, Lead, We are Made of Chemicals, A
Future Filled with Phosphates, and Idle

Door County's shoreline never fails to amaze me.
Every stretch is different—from Otumba's soft,
golden sand to La Salle Park's perfectly smooth
pebbles to Potawatomi State Park's rough, jagged
rocks. None are completely the same, but in all
places, the land meets the water meets the air.
When I stand on the edge of all three, I am
reminded that my actions impact not only myself
but also this wonderful community, and I need to
care for it, for future generations will face the
consequences of my neglect.

Zoey Kohler
Format Editor
Contributions: Insignificant Moths, Monumental Issues and How I Wonder Where You Are

Home is where the heart is; for me, this is Door County. I grew up surrounded by friendly people and entrancing nature. My favorite time of year is the first snowfall, once a thin dusting of sparkly, white powder coats the landscape. I love the fortune of taking a brisk walk in the park, bundled up with a scarf and mittens, and searching for tiny animal prints trailed in the snow. I hope future generations will also hold the opportunity to enjoy Door County's picturesque snow-covered scenery.

Emily Koelpien
Arts Editor
Contributions: Where My Soul Lives, Saving Sunshine, Black and White, Sunken Treasure, and Save Our Sister

I discovered my love for nature by walking the Ahnapee Trail. I love how everywhere you are, nature is present. Whether it's the ever-changing trees or escaping to one of the many picturesque beaches along Lake Michigan, the interconnectedness of nature along with historic towns creates a unique place to live. It's important to me that we work to preserve Door County's environment because nature is what makes Door County magical. By treating nature with respect, I energize it, and it energizes me. I am simply inspired when I'm outside in nature.

Megan Neubauer
Contributions: The Environmental Declaration of
the Citizens of Door County and Vehicular Air
Pollution: A Major Mist-dimeanor

My appreciation for where I live began when I
started to experience the world outside Door
County. I've traveled all over the continental United
States, giving me the pleasure of experiencing
environments similar to and drastically different
from Door County. The beauty of a rocky peninsula
surrounded by pristine, fresh water is a sight I hold
dear to my heart. To know that I've made a
difference through words in Door County's
environment gives me hope that generations from
now, my great-great grandchildren will enjoy the
same Door County I did.

Erin Tadych
Contributions: Nature's Necessities, Quality over Quantity, and Mortified

The skies of Door County capture my gaze every day and night. From subtle pastels to vividly stained skylines, sunrises are absolutely breathtaking as they stretch across the horizon. I often find myself perched at Potawatomi Park to watch the sun rise out of the water and into the sky. As the sun goes down, I love to watch the blue sky pop with color followed by the dazzle of sparkling stars. Every hour, the sky is alluringly different. It's important to keep Door County's air and light pollution minimal to preserve each brilliant and beautiful sky.

Olivia Van Den Heuvel
Contribution: We Are the Solution

Whenever I tell someone where I live, wide eyes of disbelief are usually followed by a smile of enthusiasm. Within seconds, the questioner inquires " DO YOU REALLY LIVE IN DOOR COUNTY, WI ?!" This, I proudly confirm as the truth. I love Door County 365 days a year, but climate change will demolish its beautiful terrain. Climate change is not an opinion, it is a fact. Door County's breathtaking autumns, iconic cherry trees and every other tourist attraction in between rely on a healthy environment, and I am not willing to give up my year round vacation home. Preserving Door County's health is preserving her beauty, and that's why I am a part of this book.

Hanna Pierre
Contributions: The Door's Deer Damage and
Goodbye, Door County

Door County feels like home. Not only do the most
friendly and welcoming people reside here, but the
natural beauty never fails to astound. Each season
captures the peace and serenity that represent Door
County. The vivid autumn leaves, the still blue
waters in summertime, and the stunning winter
wonderlands forever please its residents. Take a
stroll through your driveway as orange leaves land
beside you. Gaze at the greenery on an August bike
ride and hear the birds sing. Snowshoe through the
marvelous woodlands. The natural beauty that
Door County offers perfects the homey sentiment it
maintains, and it's our job to protect it!

Emma Jeanquart
Contribution: Plague of Impassivity

My heart belongs to Door County. Every time its beauty captivates me, I feel incredibly blessed; thinking only of how lucky I am to grow up in such perfection. Through the charm of this peninsula, symptoms of death are surfacing. Our beautiful home is attacked by negligence—with the pristine shores being littered with trash and ecosystems being bombarded with farming chemicals, it's slowly being destroyed. I, for one, cannot stand by as my home is slowly destroyed, the home I hope my family will also live in.

Anna Lebrun
Contribution: A Miracle

Door County has been home for all my life. I love spring and summer days when birds outside my window wake me every morning and lull me to sleep every night. Home to many native birds, my area, Sturgeon Bay, tries to create habitats, monitor bird migration in and out, and protect all birds, qualifying it as an official bird city.The birds in the sky and the water create an unforgettable atmosphere to tourists and residents. One of the most scenic and soundful places in Wisconsin, I wish to preserve Door County's legacy for the future to enjoy.

Regan Norton
Contribution: Environmental Laws in Door County

Hues of green fading to auburn are emphasized by the glistening of blue-green water, painting a picture of the place I call home. The art of Potawatomi State Park wraps around its twisty roads like Monet's water lilies, and there is a new stroke of beauty everywhere you look. Standing atop the tower, the view extends for miles. Door County paints this natural beauty, as well as many others all across the area, all the way to the very tip of the peninsula. This county is not only a home, but an individual in itself, an artist.

Tehya Bertrand
Contribution: Forests Today, Zero Tomorrow

When I think of Door County, I visualize an abundance of nature during fall—the trees turning bright red, hunting orange, and sun yellow. When I see them, I get lost in nature. I see the different species roaming the land, squirrels collecting nuts for winter, deer running away from hunters, and birds getting ready to leave for the south. Seeing all of these animals makes me feel like I live in an environment not found anywhere else. I love the beauty of nature we have here in Door County.

Maggie Grota
Contribution: Genetically Modified Organisms

Lake Michigan has always been a place for me to relax and enjoy nature. The crashing of waves on the sand beach, the squawking of seagulls, and the fresh air helps me escape the busyness of my daily life and simply appreciate the beauty of nature. On hot summer days, the cool waves invite swimming or running on the beach, and in winter, it transforms into a barren arctic landscape—beautiful in its own way. Whatever the season, Lake Michigan is a great place to admire the natural beauty of Door County.

Shaina Skaletski
Contribution: Harmful Habits, Sinful Cycle

It's morning, it's dark, I'm tired and lacking any possible energy to pursue my day. I trudge to my car with half open eyes and slowly back out. Fumbling for my mittens, I take a deep breath and gather the most precise focus I can to drive forward. Energy is gradually gained with each stop, acceleration, and merge. Suddenly, making my way up the bridge, it emerges. A warm, glowing sunrise reflecting onto the cracked ice with rays illuminating the water underneath. Stamina builds with increasing incline and sun rays. Gratefulness meets my new found momentum as I descend down the hill. It's an incredible privilege to see such beauty every morning and live in the joyus county that provides it, Door County.

Alex Quigley
Contribution: Natural vs. Synthetic

My favorite aspect of Door County is Cave Point—a park that attracts many spectators, including my family, wishing to see the beauty of rock formations. It consists of deep caverns along the water line, plants intertwining their roots within even the smallest crevices, and rock shelves suitable for walking on and observing Door County's natural beauty. When I'm there experiencing the cool mist of the waves crashing up against the rocks, I wonder: how can something so forceful and loud be so refreshing and rejuvenating? To me, it's because of the cool mist on my face, the thoughts of summertime on the beach with family, or having a family get-together along Door County's many shores.

Helen Parks

Contribution: Zero Waste: Eliminating—Not Minimizing—the Problem

The serene and natural Door County has been my home for 16 years. Every year, I find more beauty in every place I explore through the wondrous seasons guaranteed in Door County. I love to witness mother nature's creation while riding my horses on the trails throughout the county. Each season features amazing scenery for everyone to appreciate: the bright fall leaves, ripe, red, summer cherries, huge drifts of snow in the winter, and pops of colorful spring flowers. These aspects make Door County my favorite place to live.

Eli Jeanquart
Contribution: Aquatic Hitchhikers

Door County, the thumb of Wisconsin, is to me that one, special place called home. It is a home that is as hospitable as it is generous, bringing golden warmth that gives way to numbing cold as the seasons come and go in a continuous cycle. A home where in the summer the cherries are as delicious as they are plentiful and the waves lapping against the shoreline are more dazzling and exquisite than anywhere else. Door County: the place I can call home.

Grace LeGrave
Contribution: The Cancer of Our Ash Trees

I have never experienced beauty like Door County's. The sun-filled beaches in summer, the vivacious tree colors in fall, the snow covered evergreens in winter, and the blooming flowers in spring bring about beauty no matter the season. I love summer in Door County because of all it has to offer, especially camping. My fondest memories of camping are the competitive scavenger hunts with my cousins. I would scavenge through the rocky beaches for a piece of driftwood, go for a walks on the trails to find acorns, or examine the rocky coast for a fossil. Door County has much to offer and I'm glad I'm here to experience its beauty whenever I want.

MaCayla Moore
Contribution: No Trees, No Cherries

The blissful feeling of warm sunshine seeping through my skin, the rays spreading a tingling heat across my body—this feeling results from my favorite season, summer. After a long winter, summer is a godsend. The aromas of fresh fruits and vegetables, the brightness of laughter linger within the air, but most importantly, overdue sunlight abounds. One of my favorite aspects is tasting the various cherries that hang upon viridescent trees. Their bursting flavor reminds me of my childhood memories of playing in the orchard upon the hill. I strongly believe that my happiness lies within the memories of Door County.

Elyse Columb
Contribution: The Honey Bee

A place that has always soothed me is the water. When I think about the refreshing waves of the bay or the distinct odor of algae, it brings me to a place within my mind where I can just let go. Activities such as water skiing or swimming distract me from the stress of the world and bring me comfort. The sight of the sun reflecting off the water brings contentment, and the feeling of water hitting my skin relaxes me. Luckily for me, Door County is surrounded almost completely by water and I couldn't be more grateful.

Seth Hanson
Contribution: Solar Energy: The Choice for Door County

Door County in summer is one of the most robust places on earth. It is a place where the forests and fields fill up with hundreds of different species of plants and animals. A place where you can fish, hike, and everything in between. A place where peaceful rivers and streams connect to the open waters of Lake Michigan and Green Bay. From the hard-working farmers of Southern Door to the idyllic bustle of its northern villages or the quiet solitude of places like Rock Island, you will be hard-pressed to find a place with more variety than Door County in the summer.

Lexi Wery
Contribution: The Power of Wind

Because of its diversity, the beauty of Door County cannot be summed up in one word; however, it can be associated with one thing—nature. To me, nothing compares to the sense of belonging or liveliness Door County's natural environment cultivates in me. Though I marvel at city life, I am more than content stepping into my backyard, breathing fresh air, hearing a bird overhead, and seeing blue waters in the distance. The natural beauty of Door County, my home, is something I cherish and seek to preserve.

Alexis Jandrin
Contribution: Pesticide Use in Lawn Care

When I think of Door County, I picture the warm
summer glow the sun gives the land, I picture the
woods behind my house full of massive green trees,
I picture a garden packed with delicious harvest
waiting to be eaten, I picture my siblings and I
playing in the creek to cool down. In the summer, I
spend endless days on my grandparents farm,
helping them with their fieldwork and taking care of
all their animals. This is what I visualize when I
think about Door County.

Ben Kielar
Contribution: Microplastics in Lake Michigan

The best thing about Door County is how untouched it remains. Thousands of people live here, yet nature is prevalent wherever you go. It's no wonder Door County has become a bustling tourist destination. Wisconsin experiences four distinct seasons and has an abundance of beautiful parks and wildlife reserves to explore. I'm fortunate to have grown up here and to have experienced the many aspects of Door County that make it unique.

Anna Meier
Contribution: The Threat of Man-Made Drought

My favorite aspect of Door County is the parks. The parks are nature retreats offering endless enjoyment for locals and visitors alike. I have spent hours at them with my family, swimming, climbing trees and rocks, and enjoying the beautiful vistas. To me, protecting Door County's environment so that more people can enjoy the natural beauty of them and connect with nature is key to enjoying Door County myself.

Citations

Land

Environmental Laws in Door County
Carson, Rachel. *Silent Spring*. 2002.
Door County Environmental Council. 2016.
Teichtler, John. "Saniarian." *Door County,
        Wisconsin*.

We Are the Solution
"2017 Best Places to Live in Door County." *Niche*.
        Niche, 2018.
Schreckinger, Ben. "Trump acknowledges climate
        change — at his golf course." *POLITICO*.
        POLITICO LLC, 23 May 2016.
"Top Things to Do in Door County." *Midwest
        Living*. Meredith Corporation, 2017.
"Welcome to Door County." *Door County Visitor
        Bureau*.
"World Biomes." *KDE Santa Barbara*. Kids Do
        Ecology, 2004.

Forests Today, Zero Tomorrow
Clark, Fred, and Lisa Thomas. "Door County
        Comprehensive Forest Plan." *Wisconsin
        Healthy Forest Pilot Program*. Feb. 2007.

Clay, Tom. "Our History – Door County Land
        Trust." *Door County Land Trust.* 2018.
Frelich, Lee E. "Are These the Last Days for Door
        County's Boreal Forests?" *Door County
        Pulse.* Door County Pulse, 17 Feb. 2017.
Henry, Joe. "Baileys Harbor Boreal Forest and
        Wetlands," Tier 3 Management Plan.
        Wisconsin DNR. 28 June 2017.
Lukes, Roy, and Charlotte Lukes. "Old-Growth
        Forests." *Door County Pulse.* Door County
        Pulse, 5 Aug. 2015.
Marjanovic, Ines. "Increasing of Food Production Is
        Possible Without Deforestation." *Agrivi.*
        Agrivi, 8 Sept. 2016.
Meyer, Thomas. "Bailey's Harbor Boreal Forest And
        Wetlands" *Wisconsin Department of
        Natural Resources.* Wisconsin DNR, 19 Oct.
        2017.
Schneider, Michael, and Jens Jensen. "The Clearing
        Folk School." *The Clearing.*

Genetically Modified Organisms
Cassidy, Emily. "Are GMOs Bad for the
        Environment?" *EWG.* Environmental
        Working Group, 9 Mar. 2016.
DCEC Newsletter. Door County Environmental
        Council, 2013.
Glass, Emily. "The Environmental Impact of
        GMOs." *One Green Planet.* 2 Aug. 2013.

"GMO Facts." *Non-GMO Project*, The Non-GMO
      Project, 2016.
Jankowski, Melissa. "How Does Your Garden
      Grow?" *Door County Pulse*. Door County
      Pulse, 1 July 2006.
Landrigan, Philip J, and Charles Benbrook. "GMOs,
      Herbicides, and Public Health" *The New
      England Journal of Medicine*.
      Massachussetts Medical Society, 20 Aug.
      2015.
Shireen. "Another Strike Against GMOs – The
      Creation of Superbugs and Superweeds."
      GMO Inside. GMO Inside of Green America,
      31 Mar. 2014.
"The Community's Garden." *The Community's
      Garden*. Fox Valley Web Design LLC.
Welter, Liz. "Sturgeon Bay Considers Beekeeping
      Ordinance." *Green Bay Press Gazette*. USA
      Today Network, 2 June 2017.
"Wisconsin Ag News- Acreage." *United States
      Department of Agriculture*. USDA, 20 June
      2015.

Mortified
"Groundwater Contamination Susceptibility Map."
      *Protecting Wisconsin's Groundwater
      Through Comprehensive Planning*.
Leber, Rebecca. "Climate Change Is Already
      Causing Asthma. Cancer Too." *New
      Republic*. 7 May 2014.

McEwen, Bruce S. "Effects of Stress on the
     Developing Brain." *The DANA Foundation.*
     The Dana Foundation, 1 Mar. 2011.
Springfels, Cheryl. "Cleaner Air : Gas Mower
     Pollution Facts." *People Powered Machines.*
     PPM, 2008.
"The Causes and Effects of Groundwater
     Contamination." *All About Water Filters.* All
     About Water Filters, 20 Apr. 2017.
"The Link between the Environment and Our
     Health." *Scientific American.* Nature
     America, 2018.
"What Is Hepatitis?" *World Health Organization.*
     World Health Organization, July 2016.
Williams, Florence. "This Is Your Brain on Nature."
     National Geographic. National Geographic
     Society, 7 June 2017.

Harmful Habits, Sinful Cycle
Buff, Shelia. "What Is Dysentery and How Is It
     Treated?" *Healthline.* Healthline Media, 27
     June 2017.

Natural vs. Synthetic
"72 Uses For Common Natural Products That Save
     Money & Avoid Toxins." *Home Healthy
     Habits.* Home Healthy Habits, 15 Sept. 2016.
"Antioxidants" *Medline Plus.* Medline Plus, 11 Jan.
     2018.

"Bad Hair Day: Are Aerosols Still Bad for the Ozone
	Layer?" *Scientific American*. Nature
	America, 2018.
Braun, Perrin. "Are 'Natural' Foods Better than
	'Artificial' Foods?" *Inside Tracker*. Segterra,
	2 Jan. 2013.
Bray, Karina. "Natural and Organic Cosmetics."
	Choice. Choice Australia, 5 Aug. 2015.
"Dangers of Bleach." *Educating Wellness*.
	Educating Wellness, 2012.
Hoff, Victoria. "The Difference Between Natural,
	Organic, and Synthetic-Free Beauty
	Products." *Byrdie*. Byrdie, 26 Apr. 2017.
Jikomes, Nick. "CBD and the Brain: What Does It
	Do and What Is It Good For?" *Leafly*. 10 Oct.
	2016.
Karimi, Ali, et al. "Herbal versus synthetic drugs;
	beliefs and facts." *Journal of
	Nephropharmacology*. PMC, 1 Jan, 2015.
"Modern Essentials: a Contemporary Guide to the
	Therapeutic Use of Essential Oils."
	AromaTools, 2016.
"Pain." National Institute on Drug Abuse. NIDA, 1
	Oct. 2014.
Reeser, Dorea. "Natural versus Synthetic Chemicals
	Is a Gray Matter." *Scientific American*.
	Scientific American, 10 Apr. 2013.
"The Problem with Pesticides." *Toxics Action
	Center*. Toxic Action Center, 2015
"Types of Certification." *Soil Association*. 2017.

Zero Waste: Eliminating–Not Minimizing–the
Problem

Bordeau, Bob. "City of Sturgeon Bay Guide to Single
        Stream Recycling And Solid Waste for
        Residential Properties." 2017.

Bowen, Lauren. "3 Ways a Zero Waste Lifestyle Can
        Improve Your Health." *Care2.* Care2, 27 Oct.
        2017.

"Drinking Water Contamination by Dumps and
        Landfills." *ExtoxNet FAQs.* UCD
        EXTOXNET, Nov. 1997.

Good, Kate. "10 Ways to Adopt a Zero Waste
        Lifestyle." *One Green Planet.* 31 Jan. 2016.

"Important Things to Know About Landfill Gas."
        Department of Health. New York State.

Kathryn. "Top 10 to Get Started." *Going Zero
        Waste.* 29 Dec. 2015.

Knoblauch, Jessica A. "Plastic Not-So-Fantastic:
        How the Versatile Material Harms the
        Environment and Human Health." *Scientific
        American.* Nature America, 2 July 2009.

"Landfill Problems." *We Green-USA.*

"Moving Northeast Wisconsin Toward Zero Waste."
        Clean Water Action Council. Clean Water
        Action Council, 2018.

Simmons, Ann M. "The World's Trash Crisis, and
        Why Many Americans Are Oblivious." *Los
        Angeles Times.* Los Angeles Times, 22 Apr.
        2016.

"What Is Zero Waste?" *GrassRoots Recycling Network.* Grass Roots, 19 July 2011.

"Zero Waste: A Realistic Sustainability Program for Schools." *Environmental Education in Wisconsin.* Wisconsin Green Schools Network.

Aquatic Hitchkikers

"Great Lakes Fishery Commission." *Great Lakes Fishery Commission.*

"Invasive Species Zebra Mussels Threaten Water Quality, Fishing Industry." *Door County Pulse.* Door County Pulse, 28 Mar. 2016.

"It's No Fish Tale… Charter Boat Captain Is Living His Dream." *Wisconsin Life.* 1 Mar.

"Sea Lamprey and Control Efforts in Wisconsin." *Wisconsin Department of Natural Resources.* DNR.

"Sea Lamprey Decline In Lake Michigan, On The Rise In Lake Superior." *Wisconsin Public Radio.* 6 Oct. 2017.

"Zebra Mussels" *Wisconsin Department of Natural Resources.* DNR.

Insignificant Moths, Monumental Issues

Diss, Andrea. "Containing gypsy moth." *Wisconsin Natural Resources.* Wisconsin Department of Natural Resources, Aug. 1998.

McManus, M., et al. "Gypsy Moth." *United States Department of Agriculture.* Aug. 1992.

McNee, B. "Gypsy Moth: Unwelcome in Wisconsin."
    Wisconsin Gypsy Moth. 2010.

The Cancer of Our Ash Trees

Bergquist, Lee. "Emerald Ash Borer Found in Door
    County." *Journal Sentinel.* The Milwaukee
    Journal Sentinel, 10 June 2014.
Devlin, Peter J. "Door County Ash Die-off Could Be
    Underway." *Press Gazette Media.* Wisconsin,
    04 Sept. 2015.
"Emerald Ash Borer Management Workshop."
    Wisconsin Public Radio, Wisconsin Public
    Radio, 24 May 2017.
"Emerald Ash Borer." *Emerald Ash Borer.* Iowa
    State University.
Hubbard, Amanda. "NCFS." *North Carolina Forest
    Service.* 17 Jan. 2017.
Kovarik, Terry. "Emerald Ash Borer Detected in
    Door County." *WEAREGREENBAY.*
    WEAREGREENBAY, 11 June 2014.
Murrauy, Patty. "Emerald Ash Borer Eating Its Way
    Through Door County." *Wisconsin Public
    Radio.* Wisconsin Public Radio, 26 Apr.
    2017.
Welter, Liz. "Emerald Ash Borer Destroying Door
    Co. Trees." *Press Gazette Media.* Green Bay
    Press Gazette, 11 Apr. 2017.

The Legend of the Orchid

Dippel, Beth. "When the Dust Bowl Hit
        Sheboygan." *Sheboygan Press Media*.
        Sheboygan Press, 2 Apr. 2016.
"Old Growth" *Wisconsin Natural Resources
        Magazine*. Wisconsin Department of Natural
        Resources, Oct. 2004.
"Our History." *Door County Visitor Bureau*.
"Potawatami State Park." *Wisconsin State Parks*.
        Wisconsin Department of Natural
        Resources.
"Researchers Use 3D Printing to Learn How
        Orchids Are Tricking Insects." *3DPrint.Com*.
        Additive Manufacturing, 25 Feb. 2016.

The Honey Bee
"Bee and Honey." *United States Department of
        Agriculture*. USDA, 21 Dec. 2017.
Bessin, Ric. "Varroa Mites Infesting Honey Bee
        Colonies." *College of Agriculture, Food and
        Environment*. University of Kentucky.
"Door County Beekeepers Club." *Door County
        Beekeepers Club*.
Hopwood, Jennifer, et al. "Neonicotinoids." *The
        Xerces Society*. Xerces Society.
"How Do Bees Make Honey?" *BuzzAboutBees.net*.
        2018.
Schubert, David. "How Pesticides Are Killing the
        Bees." *CNN*. Cable News Network, 15 June
        2015.

No Trees, No Cherries

Hadley, Debbie. "10 Reasons Aphids Don't Suck." *ThoughtCo*, ThoughtCo.

Karen. "Eight Interesting Facts about Aphids and Suggestions for Control." *Karen's Garden Tips*. KarenGardenTips, 17 Mar. 2010.

Spangler, Teo. "Diseases Of Cherry Trees – What To Do When A Cherry Tree Looks Sick." *Gardening Know How*, Gardening Know How, 23 June 2016.

Verble, Mark. *Arboristsite.com*. Arborist, 2017.

The Door's Deer Damage

Alexander, Jeff. "Antlerless-Only Deer Hunting Appears Likely in Door County." *WBAY*. Gray Digital Media, 11 Apr. 2017.

Jones, Meg. "Wisconsin 6th worst in car-deer crashes." *Journal Sentinel*. The Milwaukee Journal Sentinel, 20 Sept. 2016,

Mere, R.J. "Deer overpopulation is a serious problem." *Seacoastonline.com*. Seacoastonline.com, 22 Oct. 2008.

Parr, Jackson. "Deer Collisions and How to Avoid Them." *Door County Pulse*. Door County Pulse, 30 Oct. 2015.

Peterson, Eric. "Deer Hunt 2017: Door County plans to manage its herd." *Fox 11 News*.

"Reports of Lyme Disease in Door County, Wisconsin." *TickCheck*. Centers for Disease Control and Prevention, 2018.

Zeiger, John. "Deer vs. the Environment." *On Earth.*
Natural Resources Defense Council, 8 Nov.
2008.

Air

Solar Energy: The Choice for Door County
Hahn, Dan. "How to Calculate the Amount of
Kilowatt Hours (KWh) Your Solar Panel
System Will Produce." *Solar Power Rocks.*
Proctor, Cathy. "How Many Acres of Solar Panels
Do 1,000 Homes Need?" *Denver Business
Journal.* American City Business Journals,
31 July 2013.
"Sunlight." *Wikipedia*, Wikimedia Foundation, 18
Nov. 2017, en.wikipedia.org/wiki/Sunlight.
Welter, Liz. "Waseda Farms in Door County Plugs
into New Energy Source with Solar Power."
Green Bay Press Gazette. Press Gazette
Media, 12 Sept. 2017.

Saving Sunshine
Craig, Courtney. "How to Go Solar in Your
Apartment." *Apartment Guide.* Rent Path, 6
Nov. 2013.
Glaser, P.E. "Satellite Solar Power Station." *Solar
Energy.* Pergamon, 5 Aug. 2003.
Sherwood, Chris. "Bad Things About Solar Panels."
LIVESTRONG. Leaf Group, 13 June 2017.

"Solar Power Does Work in Oregon &
        Washington?" *Sunbridge Solar*. 2018.

The Power of Wind
"Advantages and Challenges of Wind Energy."
        *Office of Energy Efficiency & Renewable
        Energy*. US Department of Energy.
Chamberlin, Rick. "Years Later, Wisconsin Wind
        Farm Fears Fail to Materialize." *Midwest
        Energy News*. Midwest Energy News, 20
        Dec. 2011.
"Door County Weather." *USA.com*. World Media
        Group, LLC, 2013.
"Rosiere Wind Farm." *MGE*. Madison Gas and
        Electric Company, 2018.
"Wind Power Pays $222 Million a Year to Rural
        Landowners." *AWEA*. American Wind
        Energy Association, 22 Mar. 2016.

Goodbye, Door County
Frantz, Vickie. "How Does the Weather Affect the
        Color of Fall Leaves?" *AccuWeather*.
        AccuWeather, 31 Aug. 2016.
"Weather History for KSUE - January, 1945."
        Weather Underground. The Weather
        Company, 2018.
Welter, Liz. "Record-breaking rainfall inundates Door
        County." *Green Bay Press Gazette*. Press
        Gazette Media, 25 July 2017.

Vehicular Air Pollution: A Major Mist-demeanor

"Air toxics and mercury." *Wisconsin DNR.*
Wisconsin Department of Natural
Resources, 24 Oct. 2017.
Devlin, Peter J. "EPA Air-Quality Concerns Reach
Door County." *Green Bay Press Gazette.*
Press Gazette Media, 31 Jan. 2017.
Hawthorne, Michael. "Smog Follows Chicagoans on
Vacation to Wisconsin, Michigan."*Chicago
Tribune.* 4 Aug. 2017.
"Tourism Spending Up 14.6 Million in Door County
Last Year." *Door County Visitor Bureau.* 1
May 2015.
"Vehicles." *Wisconsin DNR.* Wisconsin Department
of Natural Resources, 28 Sept. 2017.

How I Wonder Where You Are

Bergquist, Lee. "Newport State Park Designated as
Wisconsin's First 'Dark Sky' Park." *Journal
Sentinel.* The Milwaukee Journal Sentinel, 7
June 2017.
Berkley, Kent. "Door County must pay attention to
light pollution prevention." *Door County
Daily News.* Nicolet Broadcasting, 28 Nov.
2017.
"Door County's Internationally Recognized Dark
Sky." *Door County.* Door County Visitor
Bureau, 2018.
Fischer, Adelheid. "Starry Night." *Places Journal.*
Places Journal, June 2018.

"Preserving the Night Sky." *Door County Pulse*.
Door County Pulse, 5 Aug. 2015.
Rinkesh. "15 Impressive Ways to Reduce Light
Pollution." *Conserve Energy Future*.
Conserve Energy Future, 2018.
Skiba, Alyssa. "The Dark Ranger: Dark Sky
Advocate to Visit Door County." *Door
County Pulse*. Door County Pulse, 16 Sept.
2016.

Water

Hydrargyrum
Granholm, Jennifer M., and Janet Olszewski.
"Mercury Spill Fact Sheet." *Michigan
Department of Community Health*.
Michigan Department of Community Health.
Hintzen, Katy. "Mercury Still a Danger in the Great
Lakes." *MSU Extension*. Michigan State
University Extension, 16 Dec. 2015.

Pesticide Use in Lawn Care
"Cancer." *Pesticide Action Network*. Pesticide
Action Network North America.
Chason, Rachel. "Court Strikes down Montgomery
County's Ban on Lawn Pesticides." *The
Washington Post*. The Washington Post, 3
Aug. 2017.
"Chemicals Implicated." *Beyond Pesticides*.

Dannhausen Jr., Myles. "Making Door County
          Lawns Safer." *Door County Pulse*. Door
          County Pulse, 24 Apr. 2016.
"Environmental Impacts." *Pesticide Action
          Network*. Pesticide Action Network North
          America.
"Safe Lawns in Door County." *Door Property
          Owners*. Door Property Owners, 2018.

Reeking Havoc in Our H2O
"Health." *Sperling's*. Sperling's Best Places, 2018.
 Seely, Ron. "Bacteria in State's Drinking Water Is
          'Public Health Crisis.'" *Wisconsin Watch*.
          WisconsinWatch.org, 1 May 2016.
"Sources of Drinking Water." *Protecting
          Wisconsin's Groundwater Through
          Comprehensive Planning*. 15 Jan. 2008.

Microplastics in Lake Michigan
"An Update on Microfiber Pollution." *The Cleanest
          Line*. 3 Feb. 2017.
Andrew, Elise. "Microbeads In Soaps Facing Bans
          Due To Great Lakes Pollution." *IFLScience*.
          IFLScience, 15 Aug. 2016.
Evans, Ian. "Great Lakes Hazard: Tiny Bits of
          Plastic." *Undark*. 21 Sept. 2016,
"Great Lakes Teeming with Tiny Plastic Fibers,
          Scientists Say." *Chicago Tribune*. Chicago
          Tribune, 10 Jan. 2015.

Gross, Bob. "Plastic Microbead Pollution a Concern in Great Lakes." *The Times Herald.* Times Herald, 16 Mar. 2015.

Hamrén, Henrik. "Microplastics in Marine Animals." *Baltic Eye.* Stockholm University, 8 May 2017.

Harvey, Fiona. "Microplastics Killing Fish before They Reach Reproductive Age, Study Finds." *The Guardian.* Guardian News and Media, 2 June 2016.

Hawthorne, Michael. "A New Pollution Worry for Lake Michigan: Tiny Plastic Fibers." *Chicago Tribune.* 25 May 2016.

Humphries, Courtney. "Freshwater's Macro Microplastic Problem." *PBS.* Public Broadcasting Service, 11 May 2017.

Johnson, Todd. "How Polypropylene Plastics Affect Your Daily Life." *ThoughtCo.* 8 Sept. 2017.

Rochman, Chelsea M., et al. "Ingested Plastic Transfers Hazardous Chemicals to Fish and Induces Hepatic Stress." *Nature News.* Nature Publishing Group, 21 Nov. 2013.

Rogers, Tony. "Everything You Need To Know About Polyethylene (PE)." *Creative Mechanisms.*

Weber, Kristianna. "Micro-Plastics Are a Mega Problem for Marine Animals – Here's What We Can Do!" *One Green Planet.* 25 Oct. 2016.

"What Are PCBs?" *National Ocean Service.*
    National Oceanic and Atmospheric
    Administration of U.S. Department of
    Commerce, 10 Oct. 2017.
Zukowski, Dan. "22 Million Pounds of Plastic
    Enters Great Lakes Each Year." *EcoWatch.*
    EcoWatch, 21 Dec. 2016.

Living with CAFOs: It's a Crap Chute
Bergquist, Lee. "Massive Dairy Farms and Locals
    Debate: Can Manure from so Many Cattle Be
    Safely Spread on the Land?" *Journal
    Sentinel.* The Milwaukee Journal Sentinel,
    22 Apr. 2017.
"Centers for Disease Control and Prevention."
    Centers for Disease Control and Prevention.
    26 Apr. 2017.
Fischer, David B. "Energy Aspects of Manure
    Management." *Dairy Cattle.* University of
    Illinois Board of Trustees, 6 Aug. 1998.
Kinnard Farms. Kinnard Farms, 2018.
"Pathogen." *Merriam-Webster.* Merriam-Webster,
    15 Feb. 2018.
The National Agricultural Law Center. The
    National Agricultural Law Center of the
    University of Arkansas, 2018.
USDA. NASS and Census of Agriculture, 2018.
"Wisconsin's 2016 impaired waters list." *Wisconsin
    Department of Natural Resources.* DNR,
    2016.

The Threat of Man-Made Drought

"A blanket around the Earth." *NASA*. California
     Institute of Technology, 23 Feb. 2018.

"Climate Change & The Jet Stream." *Climate Central.*
     Climate Central, 1 Nov. 2013.

Dannhausen Jr., Myles. "Clearing the Virgin
     Forests: Door County's Logging Past." *Door
     County Pulse.* Door County Pulse, 1 May
     2005.

"Ground Water and Water Wells – Definitons and
     Explanations." *American Ground Water
     Trust.* The American Ground Water Trust,
     2016.

"Guide: What is drought and how does it happen?"
     BBC. BBC, 10 Nov. 2015.

"Jet Stream Map." *Weather Underground.* The
     Weather Company, 1 Jan. 1970.

Kasper, Matt. "How Climate Change is Damaging The
     Great Lakes, With Implications For The
     Environment And The Economy." *Think
     Progess.* Think Progess, 18 Jan. 2013.

Kitchen, Elizabeth. "What are Jet Streams? Definition,
     Development, Purpose, and Importance." *Bright
     Hub.* Bright Hub, 8 June 2011.

Leng, Guoyong, et al. "Pumping water for irrigation
     likely to increase drought vulnerability in
     certain regions." *PhysOrg*. Science X
     Network, 9 Nov. 2015.

Moon, Mariella. "Man-made global warming makes
     droughts and floods more likely." *Engadget.*
     Oath Tech Network Aol, 9 Apr. 2017.
Nehring, Andrew. "Water Wars: The Man-Made
     Drought." *Citizens Against Government
     Waste.* Citizens Against Government Waste,
     18 Mar. 2016.
"Top 20 Ways to Reduce Your Carbon Footprint."
     Global Stewards. 2018.

Save Our Sister
Alexander, Dave. "Coal Ash's Effect on Lake
     Disputed." *MLive.com.* 6 June 2009.
"Arsenic in Water - Arsenic - University of Maine."
     Arsenic, University of Maine.
Carr, Tom. "On Lake Michigan, A Cleaner Coal-
     Powered Ship Ferries On." *NPR.* NPR, 31
     May 2015.
"Coal Ash Threatens Our Health and Environment."
     Clean Water Action. Clean Water Fund.
French, Jenn. "The Environmental Impacts of
     Boating." *Environmental Protection.* 27
     Mar. 2017.
Gaumnitz, Lisa. "A Beachhead for Safe Swimming."
     Wisconsin Natural Resources Magazine.
     Wisconsin Department of Natural
     Resources, June 2003.
Hu, S.M. Imamul et al. "Arsenic Contamination in
     Food-Chain: Transfer of Arsenic into Food
     Materials through Groundwater Irrigation."

PubMedCentral. U.S. National Institutes of Health's National Library of Medicine, Sept. 2006.

"Lake Michigan Haunted by Sewage, Mercury." *Environment Illinois*. 30 Oct. 2013.

Linn, Morgan. "LNG-Powered Great Lakes Freighters Could Cut Greenhouse Emissions." *Capital News Service*. Great Lakes Echo, 30 Oct. 2015.

Lundstrom, Jim. "Lifting the Curtain on Shipbuilding in Sturgeon Bay." *Door County Pulse*. Door County Pulse, 8 Mar. 2015.

"Reducing E.coli Contamination From Beaches, Rivers and Lakes." *DEQ*.

Savage, JP. "Just How Dirty Are Great Lake Freighters." *The Round River*.

"Tourism Spending Up $15 Million in Door County Last Year." *Door County Visitors Bureau*. Door County Visitors Bureau, 5 May 2017.

www.ingramcontent.com/pod-product-compliance
Lightning Source LLC
Chambersburg PA
CBHW051735250726
48659CB00001B/72